Promenades at the
Parthenon

Cornelia Hadziaslani

Photographs
Socratis Mavrommatis

*The English version of "Promenades at the Parthenon"
has been sponsored by Nana Mouskouri*

MELINA MERCOURI FOUNDATION

PHOTOGRAPHIC SOURCES

All the photographs published in the book are the work of Socratis Mavrommatis except for those provided by the organisations listed below, which we thank:

© Ecole Nationale Suprieure des Beaux-Arts (Phot. pp. 8, 9, 10, 11, 12, 14, 15, 16, 17, 18, 19, 20, 21, 26, 27, 28, 29, 30, 31).

© Birmingham City Museum and Art Gallery (Phot. pp. 18, 19, 32).

© Berlin National Gallery (Phot. pp. 34, 35).

© Musée du Louvre (Phot. pp. 107, 128, 129).

© Benaki Museum (Phot. pp. 53, 57, 78, 79).

© Gennadeios Library (Phot. pp. 51, 56).

Text Supervision: Irene Kaimara

English Translation: Miriam Caskey

Artisitic Supervision: ALTSYS

Cover Design: Socratis Mavrommatis

Publication supervision: Yiorgos Depollas

Colour separations: TOXO Co.

Printing: EPIKINONIA LTD.

Binding: Yiorgos Heliopoulos

Production-Distribution: Editions FOTORAMA Tel: 01-3643592 Fax: 01-3643323

Email: info @ fotorama.gr   Internet: www.fotorama.gr

ISBN: 960-7524-08-X

*T*he Melina Mercouri Foundation and Mr. Jules Dassin have honoured me with a request to write a book for young people about the Parthenon and its sculpture. The purpose of the book is to familiarise the readers with classical art, both architecture and sculpture, so that when they visit the Acropolis and also the British Museum, where much of the sculpture of the great temple is today, they can comprehend and appreciate it.

In the initial phase great difficulties were encountered in simplifying descriptions and references. The relation between the architecture and the sculpture, especially marked in the Parthenon, as well as the concept of the statues as a whole today is lost. By now the sculpture has become a collection of single and mutilated masterpieces. The relief of the messenger goddess Iris from the east frieze is representative of the senseless and haphazard division of the Parthenon sculpture between two museums: the head is exhibited in the Acropolis Museum and the body in the British Museum.

In order to cope with these difficulties, a mythical figure was used as narrator, Iris herself. The conventional sense of time and place was thus bypassed and the book was divided into four parts with an Epimetron. As protagonist, Iris accompanies the reader on promenades through antiquity, into history, through the monument itself and to the two museum collections. In the first part of the book Iris, the reader's guide, proudly shows him the Parthenon in its finished form, as it was when it was completed in 432 B.C. by Perikles and Pheidias. In the second part, she takes him through the historical vicissitudes of the great temple; she shows him the damage, great and lesser, sustained by the building through time to the present day. In the third and fourth parts, still beside the reader, she reminds him of the original appearance of the temple as they saw it together and she helps him to re-visualise the entire composition of the sculpture from the fragments preserved in the museums.

Thus the first chapter of the book unfolds in the world of imagination. Its title, "A Promenade into the World of Imagination," was chosen also to show that the splendid illustrations of this chapter are to a great extent products of the imagination too. They are impressive representations of the monuments, most of them by architects of the 19th century, fellows of the Ecole Nationale Suprieure des Beaux-Arts of Paris. These architects took part in the missions of the School to Athens and they produced restored drawings and paintings that reflect as much the spirit of the time as they do their own academic and personal quests.

The second chapter of the book unfolds in the realm of history. It is illustrated with historical documents and by precise restored drawings that show how this masterpiece of the ancient world deteriorated and was altered during the course of the centuries.

The next two chapters have to do with the actual state of the Parthenon today. The aim is to familiarise the reader with the monument and with the two great collections of the sculpture in Athens and in London.

Finally, the Epimetron gives a picture of all the sculpture of the Parthenon preserved, combined with the precise drawings of Jacques Carrey, who drew the sculpture in 1674 while it was still on the monument, thirteen years before the bombardment of the temple in 1687.

In the first chapter Iris recognises and describes figures that today are lost. In the subsequent chapters she describes only those figures that have been identified and interpreted by archaeological scholarship.

The book itself, I would never have been able to complete without my experience at the Acropolis where from 1987 on, I am in charge of Education of the Committee for the Preservation of the Acropolis Monuments and the Ist Ephorate of Prehistoric and Classical Antiquities. The book is a distillation of lessons given to thousands of children and educators.

The "Promenades at the Parthenon" could not have been completed without the help of many people, most of all my husband, Charalambos Bouras, chairman of the Committee for the Preservation of the Acropolis Monuments. From the Ephor of the Acropolis, Alcestis Choremi, as well as from the Honourary Ephor Evi Touloupa, I have had constant help and encouragement. I owe them all special gratitude.

The photographer, Socratis Mavrommatis, has been the basic collaborator in the book. I am indebted to him for the splendid photographs of the sculpture, the monuments themselves and the many paintings, with all the inherent difficulties of making these photographs. The extraordinarily demanding task of synthesising the elements of the Epimetron is his work as well. His advice has been invaluable in all phases of preparing the book and he has added much to its quality.

An important characteristic of the book is that it is based on a continuous connection of the pictures with the descriptions of the monuments. Thus, while the description is part of a continuous text, it is at the same time an expanded caption for the picture. The demands of page lay-out were thus enormous and I would like to express great thanks to Ina Melengoglou and Anthia Destouni-Chatzinikoli for their superb artistic supervision of a book in which each phrase had to be next to a certain illustration. I thank also Nikos Alexiadis, Giorgos Depollas and Alekos Valavanis for the edition as a whole and for their fine collaboration.

Supervision of the text was in the hands of my colleague in the educational programmes, the archaeologist Irene Kaimara, to whom I owe many thanks. She worked tirelessly through all phases of the book and her contribution was far beyond the simple overseeing of a text. Thanks go also to the archaeologists Niki Psarraki-Belesioti and Assimina Leonti for their comments.

The archaeologist Miriam Caskey made the English translation of the text with literary care. I thank her greatly, for her efforts have enhanced the book.

To Mr. Jules Dassin and the Board of Directors of the Melina Mercouri Foundation who entrusted me with the writing of the book, go special thanks. I am very grateful for the devoted cooperation of Manuella Pavlidou since without her constant encouragement and the endless hours she gave, the book would never have been finished. Likewise Paulina Tzeirani who willingly placed all the orders and collected the photographs from the various museums.

Nana Mouskouri's donation made possible the English edition of the book. We are grateful to her for her donation.

Thanks go also to Professor Manolis Korres for permission to use his drawings.
For their photographs and for photographic material, thanks are due to the Archive of the Committee for the Preservation of the Acropolis Monuments, and especially to the Keeper Fani Mallouhou-Tufano, to the Benaki Museum and especially to the Keeper of the Photographic Archive, Fani Kostantinou and to the Keeper of the N. Hadjikyriakos-Ghikas collection, Ioanna Providou, to the Gennadeios Library, to Mina Bouras, to Giorgos and Irene Rayias, to Stavros Stavridis and to Tasos Tanoulas.

All the contributors to the book are bound together with old friendship. All worked with great enthusiasm toward its completion. Friends, professionals, each with a personal tie to the monument itself, with respect for the general public, with real enthusiasm for the subject and for education, all worked in the common conviction that knowing the Parthenon should not be the privilege of just a few specialists but should be the prerogative of all. We sincerelly hope that the new Acropolis Museum will be completed soon, so that the sculptures of the great temple may be restored to their rightful place.

Cornelia Hadziaslani
September 2000

Parthenon, west pediment,
figure N. British Museum.

« Ῐρις

ἀελλόπους

χρυσόπτερος

ἀγγελέουσα

ποδήνεμος

ὠκέα »

so Homer

calls me

I am Iris, messenger of the gods, and I can assume
human or divine form as I please. I have wings, I wear winged
sandals and I carry the kerykeion, the symbol of the herald who bears
and proclaims messages. Homer sings of my wings, and he calls me «golden-
winged messenger» (χρυσόπτερος ἀγγελέουσα) and «storm-swift»
(ἀελλόπους) that is as quick as the gale, «wind-swift of foot» (ποδήνεμος ὠκέα), since my feet are fleet as the wind.

The ancient Athenians gave human form to their deities. The brilliant
sculptors of the Parthenon portrayed me in the pediment, the metopes
and the frieze as a young girl, always ready to fly off at any moment,
with my hair wind-blown and with all the characteristics of youth and
motion. I have been up here for 2,500 years. Through the ages I have
watched the visitors as they look at me. I have always longed to show the
temple to someone, just as it was when it was dedicated, with the most
beautiful sculpture that has ever been created all intact, so that the brilliance of
the dedication could be imagined, with the great temple in all its glorious detail
gleaming in the Attic light.

I have chosen you, so let's begin. Let's travel back in time so that I can show you the
Parthenon as it was when the building had just been completed, as no other of your
contemporaries has ever seen it.

Parthenon, east frieze, block V, Acropolis Museum, no. 855. Detail.

Next page:
M. Lambert. View of the west side of the Acropolis, restored drawing.
Detail. 1877, Paris, Ecole Nationale des Beaux-Arts (E.N.B.A.).

A Promenade
into the World of
Imagination

B. Loviot. Restored drawing of the east end of the Parthenon, 1879-1881, Paris, E.N.B.A.

Come and see the temple and its architecture

This is a marvelous building with its fine proportions and its perfect construction. Except for the wooden roof beneath the marble tiles, the entire temple is made of white Pentelic marble. It is enormous, being some 70 meters long, 31 meters wide and 15 meters high. The Doric columns around the exterior have a lower diameter of 1.91 meters and they are 10.50 meters high. Some 16,500 architectural pieces of marble went into the construction of the building and they are all perfectly joined to each other. It took only nine years to build it, while Perikles was in office. In those days the city of Athens had reached the pinnacle of power and was the cultural vanguard of all the ancient world. Six years after the completion of the temple, the temple sculpture too was finished.

The Parthenon was designed by two architects, Iktinos and Kallikrates. Responsible for the final appearance of the temple together with its sculptured decoration, however, was Pheidias, an extraordinarily gifted sculptor, famous for many other works as well.

In ancient Greek architecture, the architectural style or order of the temples is discerned primarily from the form of the columns and the entablature (epistyle, frieze and geison) they support. The Parthenon is a Doric temple with Ionic elements. Let us take a close look at the differences between these two orders.

P. Delaroche. Apelles with Iktinos on the right and Pheidias on the left. Detail of wall painting. «La Renommee distribuant ses recompenses,» Salle de l'Hemicycle, 1841, Paris, E.N.B.A.

The columns differ in their proportions: the Ionic are taller and slenderer, they have a different sort of capital and they have a base, which the Doric columns lack. The epistyle (architrave, or lowest member of the entablature) of the Doric order is plain, whereas in the Ionic order it comprises three superimposed sections. Directly above the epistyle is the frieze which in the Doric order is composed of triglyphs and metopes, each metope often decorated in relief. In the Ionic order, instead, the relief decoration of the frieze is continuous; uninterrupted, it runs around the entire building.

The Ionic elements of our temple are not immediately evident. They comprise the continuous frieze that runs around the outer side of the cella and the two porches, and also the four Ionic columns of the separate western compartment.

B. Loviot. Restored drawing of the east end of the Parthenon. Detail. 1879-1881, Paris, E.N.B.A.

J. Tetaz. Restored drawing of the east side of the Erechtheion. Detail. 1847-1848, Paris, E.N.B.A.

A. Paccard. Restored drawing of the south side of the Parthenon, 1879-1881, Paris, E.N.B.A.

South side

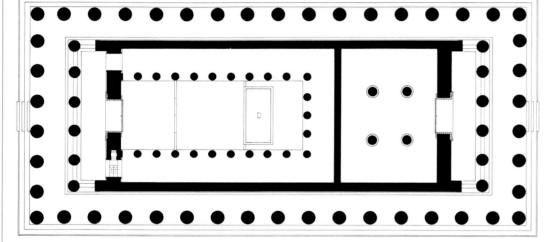

East side

West side

A. Paccard. Restored drawing of the east end of the Parthenon, 1879-1881, Paris, E.N.B.A.

Plan of the Parthenon, drawing by M. Korres.

North side

A. Paccard. Restored drawing of the long section of the Parthenon, 1879-1881, Paris, E.N.B.A.

The Parthenon is described by specialists as octastyle, peripteral, double, with a hexastyle amphiprostyle cella. Some explanation is needed so that you can understand these terms.

The temple is defined as peripteral because it is surrounded by a «pteron»; in other words it has four colonnades. It is called octastyle because at each end it has eight columns. The long sides have seventeen. Thus the exterior colonnade has a total of forty-six columns. The east end is the front of the temple.

The cella is the closed space which houses the great statue of the goddess. The temple is characterised as double because the cella is divided into two separate compartments, one at the east and one at the west, which do not communicate with each other. In the eastern room a two-tiered Doric colonnade, Π-shaped in plan, encloses the statue and supports the roof. The roof over the western room is supported by four very tall Ionic columns.

The temple is said to have a hexastyle amphiprostyle cella because at each end, within the «pteron», there is a second row of columns, likewise Doric, known as the prostasis, with six columns. The temple thus has a total of 46 + 12 = 58 columns. The space between the east prostasis and the cella forms the pronaos or east portico; the corresponding space at the west is the opisthonaos or rear portico. The peripteral colonnades, the pronaos and opisthonaos all have marble ceilings of large horizontal blocks, with coffers, square sunken panels with border mouldings of double curvature (cymatia) and a painted decoration in the centre.

A. Paccard. Restored drawing of the east end of the Parthenon, 1879-1881, Paris, E.N.B.A.

A temple comprises a base, the trunk of the building (cella and columns) and the crown (entablature and roof).

The base of the temple, the krepis or platform, is made up of three steps. Yet you must note that these three steps do not form a simple stair. They are so high that no one can climb them easily. The columns rest on the third step which is known as the stylobate because on this the columns stand (from the ancient Greek "stylos" = a support, and "baino" = stand or step on).

You do not immediately notice the subtle curvature of the steps of the krepis, on all sides of the temple. Yet if you look carefully along the steps from one corner to the other, it is, indeed, apparent. The entablature as a whole has this same curvature. This and the incline of the architectural members toward the interior of the temple, are the famous refinements of the ancient classical temple. While virtually invisible, they impart harmony and, even more, they breathe a unique liveliness into an inanimate building.

The Doric columns have a shaft and a capital. They have no separate base, but rest directly upon the stylobate. Their upper diameter is less than the lower by 15 centimeters. This difference is known as tapering or contractura and it enhances the impression of stability given by the columns. If you look carefully, you will notice that the shaft is slightly thicker just below the middle; this gradual swelling is called entasis, and it is this which makes the column seem alive. The columns have 20 flutes which end in sharp arrises (edges). The changing play of light and shadow along the fluting, as the sun moves from East to West, makes a separate entity of each column and emphasises its sculptural nature.

The most characteristic element of the column is the capital. The capital of the Doric column, which we see here, is made up of the square abacus, the echinus and the hypotrachelium (grooves beneath the necking at juncture of capital and shaft).

Detail of same.

15

The entablature comprises the epistyle, the frieze and the geison (or cornice).

Above the columns is the epistyle (literally, «on the columns») and resting on that is the frieze. In the Doric order the frieze is formed of triglyphs, which have two vertical channels and two chamfers (making three channels) and metopes. The metopes are approximately square plaques, usually decorated in relief. The geison projects markedly, thus protecting the lower members of the temple from rain.

At the two ends of the temple, the slanting roof together with the geison form a large triangle, the pediment. Within this are placed the pedimental sculptures, statues in the round which rest on the shelf of the horizontal geison.

B. Loviot. Restored drawing of the Doric Order, 1879-1881, Paris, E.N.B.A.

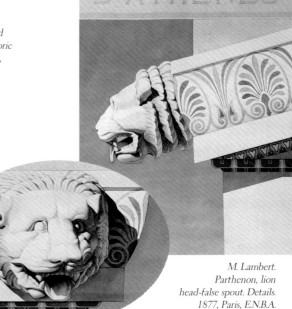

M. Lambert. Parthenon, lion head-false spout. Details. 1877, Paris, E.N.B.A.

The Parthenon has marble roof tiles. On the long sides the tiles end in a series of antefixes in the form of an anthemion. Lion-head pseudo-spouts decorate each of the four corners of the roof.

At the two ends and on the top of each pediment are the acroteria; statues in the round at the ends, with an enormous and finely carved anthemion between them at the apex.

M. Lambert. Parthenon, southwest view, as it was at that time, 1877, Paris, E.N.B.A.

ANGLE SVD-OVEST DV PARTHENON
ETAT ACTVEL AV 1/10

Come and see the sculpture of the temple

The wealth of sculptural decoration of the temple is unique. All the surfaces which, depending on their architectural composition, could be decorated, have sculptural decoration, even if this is not clearly visible to the visitor. In fact, some of the most beautiful sculptures are high up, in places that have little light and are barely visible.

You can very quickly discern three different sorts of decoration. In the pediments (marked with a green line on the plan), as we said, there are large statues in the round. On the exterior of the building, the metopes of the Doric frieze (marked with a red line) have representations in high relief; they give the impression of figures carved in the round because they protrude from the ground of the slab as much as 35 centimeters. Finally, on the Ionic frieze (marked in blue), which runs around the cella and the two hexastyle porticos, the relief is very low, with a depth of only 5 centimeters, resembling painting.

You see that all this exterior sculpture, which is carved in Pentelic marble, is coloured: the triglyphs and the background of the frieze are blue, the figures, both those in the round and the reliefs, are painted in their natural colours. The effect is enhanced by a multitude of small accessories (harnesses, weapons etc), which could not be carved in marble but are attachments in bronze, some of them gilded.

B ➡

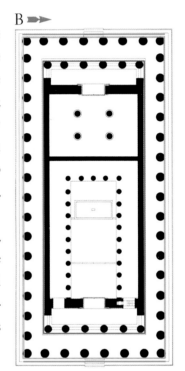

Ionic frieze.

Doric frieze (triglyphs and metopes).

L. Alma Tadema. Pheidias and the Parthenon Frieze, oil painting, 1868. Detail. Pheidias holding the plan of the temple, Birmingham, City Museum and Art Gallery.

18

Pediment.

The iconographic programme of a temple is created for political, religious and social purposes. I followed all this when the plans of the temple were worked out; when the themes for the sculpture were chosen. I followed all the discussions about the symbolism of every unit, about the relation of the themes to each other, about the way in which the iconographical units were concentrated in the statue of Athena Parthenos within the cella. The consistency of the sculptural decoration as a whole is unique. As you know from your own time, this is because the «general supervisor» was Pheidias, who was entrusted by Perikles, the initiator of the entire programme and voice of the Athenian people's will. The economic difficulties had been resolved; the funds of the Athenian Alliance were available. For the Athenians considered them to be compensation for the destruction suffered by the Acropolis at the hands of the Persians, and as just recompense for the protection they were providing to the cities that were their allies.

L. Alma Tadema. Pheidias and the Parthenon Frieze,
oil painting, 1868. Detail. Perikles,
Birmingham, City Museum and Art Gallery.

Come and see the statue of Athena Parthenos

If you ask me, now, about every single piece of sculpture, we must begin with the most wonderful, the most famous work of art on the Acropolis, the splendid chryselephantine statue of Athena Parthenos which stands to a height of 13,50 meters inside the temple cella. As you can see, it is of extraordinarily fine workmanship and its setting in the architecture of the interior space is unique.

The goddess is shown standing, armed but peaceful. She expresses wisdom, utter calmness and purity, just as she is imagined by the poets, orators, philosophers and artists, and by all mortals who worship her. This tremendous statue is impressive not only because of its form, but also because of the precious materials of which it is made: the nude parts, as you see, are of ivory and the drapery and armour of gold. Just imagine! The gold weighs as much as 1.150 kilos. Moreover the gold is «removable», that is it can be removed from the statue and used if needed by the city.

Athena wears a long peplos that falls to her feet and over that the aegis, a protective cuirass of goatskin, with the gorgoneion, the apotropaic head of Medusa on her breast. She stands on a base decorated with reliefs showing the birth of Pandora. On her shield you can see scenes from the Amazonomachy and the Gigantomachy. Her sandals have scenes from the Centauromachy and on her impressive, tall helmet there are griffins (beasts similar to lions but with wings and the beak of an eagle) and a sphinx. In one hand the goddess holds a statue of Nike (Victory) and in the other her spear; from her shield an enormous coiled snake protrudes.

Around the tremendous statue are many dedications to the goddess, especially sculpture and vases of precious metal which show how much the people respect her.

B. Loviot. Restored drawing of cross-section of Parthenon. Detail. 1879-1881, Paris, E.N.B.A.

B. Loviot. Restored drawing of long section of Parthenon. Detail. 1879-1881, Paris, E.N.B.A.

K. Schwerzek. Reconstruction of the east pediment, Acropolis Museum.

Come and see the pediments

Let's go outside of the temple again so that we can look at the two pediments. The Greek word for pediment, aetoma, comes from the word aetos which means eagle. Have you ever seen an eagle with wings outspread?

The worshippers, of course, see the pediments from the ground, that is from a distance of about 15 meters. Let's have a closer look at these fabulous statues. How large they are! The figures in their various poses, some standing, others seated, are beautifully arranged within the pedimental triangle. They rest on the horizontal geison, which is 90 centimeters wide and 28,50 meters long. The figures in the centre rise to a height of some 3,30 meters. Just look at the details of workmanship, the slanting arrangement of these vast sculptural masses, and notice also the limbs of the figures which here and there project beyond the geometrical boundaries of the architecture.

The themes of the pediments are drawn from the life of the goddess Athena. Her supernatural birth, in the presence of all the gods, is depicted in the east pediment; shown in the west pediment is the contest between Athena and Poseidon for patronage of the city, with all the heroes watching.

You must understand that the eastern end of a temple is the most sacred. At the east is the entrance and the altar where all the worshippers gather. The sculpture on the east end shows the most sacred scenes of all. The birth of Athena from the head of Zeus is indeed one of the most important events of ancient religion. Let us look at it from close up.

The composition gives an impression of symmetry even though there is no strict equivalence between the figures right and left of the main axis where the central figure of Zeus is placed. Next to him you see Athena and Hephaistos who, according to the myth, opened the head of Zeus with an axe so that the goddess could be born. Sitting next to Zeus are also Hera, Poseidon, Hermes, Ares, Apollo and Artemis. Hera wears a peplos, Athena is distinguished by her helmet and Apollo, as god of music, by his lyre.

The scene of the birth of Athena is framed at the two ends of the pediment by the figures of the rising Sun (Helios) and the setting Moon (Selene), showing that her birth took place at dawn. Helios rises from the sea; his chariot is not shown but you can see that his arms are outstretched to hold the reins of the four chariot horses. It is the same with Selene who appears to be sinking into the sea, her chariot implied by the horses' heads.

To the left, Dionysos, lying nude, with godly serenity, holds a vessel. Next are Demeter and her daughter, Kore or Persephone, seated on cube-like cases. Demeter is turning toward the scene of birth, while Kore looks straight ahead. Their poses are entirely natural and yet they fit harmoniously into the pedimental composition. Next to them Artemis moves toward the left, while looking back at the centre of the pediment.

You will notice the same in the right side. Here three seated women are shown; a group of three goddesses, Hestia, Dione and her beautiful daughter Aphrodite, who stretches out languidly in her mother's arms. The whole atmosphere breathes peace and the serenity of the Olympian divinities. The statues are all in the same style and they depict a myth that is directly connected with the goddess who is protector of the city.

Now let's have a look at the west pediment of the Parthenon.

Here too, just as in the east pediment, the poses of the figures are natural; there is stylistic unity and the figures are set in poses that accord with the triangular pedimental space. They illustrate a myth; shown here is the contest between Athena and Poseidon for possession and patronage of Attica. The scene, which the myth says took place on the Acropolis during the reign of the mythical king Kekrops, shows the heroes and the traditional ancestors of the Athenians.

The two divinities present their gifts, the «sacred testimonials», Athena her olive tree and Poseidon the spring of salt sea water. The goddess of course wins. The myth tells us that Poseidon, angered at the superiority of his opponent, inflicted floods on Attica that subsided only with the intervention of Zeus. It is this exact moment that is shown in the pediment.

Let us go for a moment to the neighbouring temple, the Erechtheion, to see these «sacred testimonials». On the western side stands the sacred olive of Athena. The Persians burned it down, yet it sprang to life again and brought forth leaves. Nearby the spring gushed out of the earth. Now look at the ceiling above the north porch and you will observe that one of the coffers is missing. It was never put in place to begin with, because beneath this was the spot that was struck by the thunder bolt of Zeus; the marks have remained on the rock.

J. Tetaz. Restored drawing of the west side of the Erechtheion, 1847-1848, Paris, E.N.B.A.

Now we shall return to the Parthenon to have a closer look at the west pediment. Left and right of the centre, the two divinities, Athena and Poseidon, compose a V with their bodies pulling away from the axis. They are framed by the two chariots that brought them to the contest, with Nike and Poseidon's wife, Amphitrite, respectively, as charioteers; they ride on waves. Together with the bronze thunderbolt of Zeus they show that the moment depicted is when Zeus interferes to stop the deluge. Various sea-monsters, tritons and dolphins shown in the pediment help to explain the myth.

The two divinities in the middle of the pediment are over life-sized, around 3,30 meters high. Athena has a spear and helmet, and she wears a peplos with the aegis obliquely across her breast. The olive tree which has sprung up beside her is of bronze; the fine twigs and leaves could never have been made in marble. Various ornaments applied to the statue are of gilded bronze. Poseidon holds his trident and is represented nude. The antithetical movement of the two central figures is brought into balance by the two pairs of horses, which the charioteers are with difficulty trying to hold in check.

We two messengers can be seen behind the chariots. I myself, Iris, on one side with Poseidon; on the other side near Athena is Hermes. We are coming to announce the desire of Zeus that the contest and the flood be ended. Hermes is running while looking back. Look at the movement of his feet; doesn't it show that he is a messenger? And likewise myself! Just see how I am running toward the centre of the scene. My great wings, set in my back, are spread wide. See the force with which I pass through the wind and run. My belt is of metal.

In the north angle is Kekrops and his daugher, Pandrossos. The child next to him is his son, Erysichthon. Sitting in the south angle is Oreithyia, the daughter of Erechtheus. She was married to the north wind, Boreas, and in the pediment her twin sons, Zetes and Kalas are beside her.

The half reclining figures in the two corners are personifications of the river Kephissos and the Kallirrhoe spring. Kallirrhoe is shown reclining on a rock, looking toward the centre toward the contest of the deities. Beside her, shown nude, sits Ilissos, the other Attic river.

Come and see the metopes

As I said, the frieze or diazoma of the Doric temple, which encircles the entire building above the architrave and beneath the geison, is made up of triglyphs and metopes. On the Parthenon all the metopes are decorated with sculpture in relief, which is unique in ancient Greek architecture. The relief is so high that if one could look at this same level along the metopes from the side, the triglyphs would not show at all and the reliefs would appear to be continuous! But the metopes are in fact slabs that were set in place by sliding them on flanges along the sides of the triglyphs. They are held in place by the geison block on top. Thus they have to be ready before the geison is put in place and the roof built. So, you can see, these are the first sculptures that were made for the temple.

The ninety-two metopes were carved on the ground and indeed by different teams of sculptors and stone-carvers who undertook separate parts of the work. Among them were settlers (metoikoi) who had come to Athens, most of them from the islands. This explains the minor differences of style seen in the metopes. Many of them were made by older, conservative artists. Yet among all these sculptors some can already be singled out for their great talent.

The themes depicted on the metopes are drawn from Greek mythology. Most of them, of course, show a subject that is always popular in ancient Greek art, the struggle. Yet look carefully at the extraordinary variety of these scenes; no single metope is like another!

A. Paccard. Restored drawing of the entablature of the Parthenon, 1845-1846, Paris, E.N.B.A.

On the east end, that is the main façade of the temple, are scenes from the Gigantomachy, the struggle of the Olympian Gods against the Giants who were trying to upset the order of the world. Except for the last metope to the right, which shows the chariot of Helios, the Sun, all the other thirteen metopes show gods, some in chariots, some on foot, fighting, each in separate battle with a giant. Most are turned toward the center of the façade, toward the metope where Zeus is portrayed. Athena, in the fourth metope from the left, is accompanied by a little Nike who is crowning her as victor.

  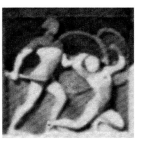  

East metope 1. Hermes.   *East metope 2. Dionysos.*   *East metope 3. Ares.*   *East metope 4. Athena.*   *East metope 5. Amphitrite.*

  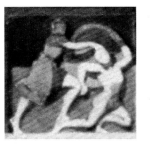  

East metope 6. Poseidon.   *East metope 7. Hera.*   *East metope 8. Zeus.*   *East metope 9. Herakles.*   *East metope 10. Artemis.*

East metope 11. Apollo and Eros.   *East metope 12. Aphrodite.*   *East metope 13. Hephaistos.*   *East metope 14. Helios with his chariot.*

A. Paccard. Restored drawing of the metopes of the east end of the Parthenon. Details from the drawing of the east end. 1879-1881, Paris, E.N.B.A.

On the opposide side, the west façade, are scenes of the Amazonomachy. Greeks, with their hero Theseus, confront the Amazons, a barbaric tribe of female warriors, who, according to the myth, lived somewhere in Pontos. Here they are shown clad in their usual dress, the short chiton, and they are fighting, some on horseback, the Greeks who are represented nude. The Queen of the Amazons, Antiope, is depicted on the first metope at the left, riding her horse.

On the north side you can see scenes from the Trojan War, especially the fall and destruction of Troy by the Greeks, a tale well-known as «The Fall of Troy». But in addition to the main theme there are mythological scenes as well, such as on the last metope at the right, which shows Athena standing in front of the seated mother of the gods, Hera. This is an extraordinary piece of sculpture. I myself, Iris, am on the next metope to the left with Zeus, the father of the gods.

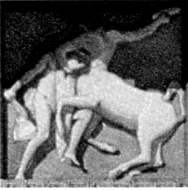
South metope 1.

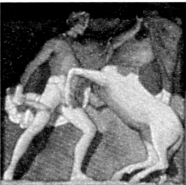
South metope 7.

The theme of twenty-three of the metopes along the south side is the Centauromachy. The other nine depict various subjects. The Thessalian Lapiths invited their neighbours the Centaurs to the wedding of their king, Peirithoos. The myth tells us that the Centaurs were a barbaric tribe with the body of a horse and torso and head of a man. At the wedding, the Centaurs had too much to drink and they tried to carry off the Lapith women. The result was a hand to hand brawl. For the Greeks, the Centauromachy symbolised the confrontation of civilisation and logic with barbarity. Among the heroes you can see Theseus, the founder of Athens, who was also, according to the myth, invited to the wedding.

F. C. Penrose. Restored drawing of the northwest corner of the Parthenon, in Principles of Athenian Architecture, London 1851.

Thus, the metopes of the Parthenon show, for the most part, four themes, known also from the sculpture of many other Greek temples and from various other works of art. These themes entail contests and struggles, the outcome of which hangs always in the balance.

South metope 2.

South metope 3.

South metope 4.

South metope 5.

South metope 8.

South metope 9.

South metope 26.

South metope 27.

South metope 28.

South metope 29.

South metope 30.

South metope 31.

B. Loviot. Restored drawing of the metopes of the south side of the Parthenon. Details from the drawing of the east end. 1879-1881, Paris, E.N.B.A.

B. Loviot. Restored drawing of the Doric Order. Detail. 1879-1881, south metope 28, Paris, E.N.B.A.

A. Paccard. Restored drawing of the entablature of the Parthenon. Detail. 1845-1846, south metope 1, Paris, E.N.B.A.

31

Come and see the frieze

L. Alma Tadema. *Pheidias and the Parthenon frieze, oil painting, 1868,*
Perikles and Aspasia visiting the Parthenon building site and Pheidias showing them the frieze, Birmingham, City Museum and Art Gallery.

Now let's go inside the colonnade so that we can see the frieze, which runs around the cella and the two porches. Do you know what the Greek word for frieze, zophoros, means? The word is made up of the noun «life» (zoe in Greek) and the verb «to bear, to carry» (fero in Greek). In fact, the frieze is a continuous band, bearing representations of people and animals moving along it. It decorates temples of the Ionic order. To put a continuous frieze like this on the Parthenon, which is of the Doric order, was a real innovation. Of course the purpose was to embellish with figures a monument the like of which has never been seen.

The frieze is twelve meters higher than the stylobate and very close to the ceiling. This means that it is not very well lit and no direct sunlight falls on it. As I mentioned before, the relief is very low and the visitor who stands outside the colonnade has trouble seeing it because it is partly hidden by the columns. Yet that does not detract from the essence of the work which is basically a splendid offering to the goddess. The rich colours and the little metal attachments which complete the reliefs, as you can see, make this a very impressive work of art.

Yet its greatest interest lies in the theme itself, which is the Panathenaic procession. The Panathenaia is the great Athenian festival celebrating the birthday of the goddess and held with special brilliance every four years. It lasts quite a few days and it includes athletic games, horseback, musical, rhapsody and other contests. The day of the goddess's birthday, on the 28th of the month Hekatombaion, that is around the 15th of your month of August, there is a big procession to the Acropolis. On that occasion the Athenians offer the goddess a new dress, the luxurious peplos that they have made for her, and they hold sacrifices in her honour.

As I have already explained to you, the iconographic programme of a temple has political, religious and social purposes. The Panathenaic procession on the Parthenon frieze depicts in a very direct way the most equitable and perfect form of government that has ever existed, Democracy. There were a number of discussions about the theme and about how it should be arranged along a length of about 160 meters. The procession, of course, had to make its way to the east end, but where should it begin? Pheidias came up with a brilliant idea: two processions would begin at the southwest corner, one moving along the west end and north side and one along the south side. In this way, the participants in the procession would 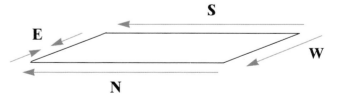 always be seen to proceed toward the east end of the temple; on the north side from right to left and on the south from left to right. The two parts of the procession would meet on the east end.

K. F. Schinkel. A look at the golden age of Greece,
copy by Wilhelm Ahlborn, Berlin, National Gallery.

34

Rendition of part of the west frieze of the Parthenon, painted by N. Hatzikyriakos-Ghikas, Benaki Museum, N. Hadzikyriakos-Ghikas Pinakotheke.

Taking part in the procession were men and women, priests with their sacred utensils, horsemen, chariots, animals for sacrifice. The gods and goddesses of Mt Olympos would watch the procession; but how should they be separated from the people? The solution was found: they would be shown on a larger scale, but seated on stools so that they would fit into the frieze. They would be placed of course on the east end. What should go in the centre? It was decided to show the moment when the peplos was offered. So, in the midst of the gods and goddesses, we see the priest, the priestess and the three children playing their part in the celebration.

This enormous sculptural entity was finished in four years. The composition includes 360 human figures and around 250 animals, most of them horses. The reliefs were outlined and carved on marble blocks 65 centimeters thick. As with the metopes, there are minor stylistic differences among them. Many sculptors worked on this frieze, perhaps at one point as many as fifty.

But let's have a really good look at the procession.

We shall follow its course, beginning at the west end. At each corner a marshall is shown and between them horsemen in various poses, scenes familiar enough to Athenians who celebrated the Panathenaia. The whole depiction, in which the figures are more widely spaced than on the other sides, is characterised by variety. The procession moves from right to left and it includes young men preparing to ride their horses with others who are already mounted.

The procession leads to a marshall and the block on which he is sculptured is at the north corner of the temple. He is in fact on the west end of the first block of the north side, looking back at the figures approaching along the west.

Let's follow the procession!

J. Stuart, N. Revett. Restored drawing of the west frieze of the Parthenon, 1751-1753, in The Antiquities of Athens, vol. II, London 1787, private collection.

J. Stuart, N. Revett. Restored drawing of sections of the north frieze of the Parthenon, 1751-1753, op. cit.

The composition of the first section of the north side comprises groups of sixty horsemen, which overlap each other on successive levels.

The next section shows the contest of the apobates. This is a contest that takes place in the celebration of the Panathenaia, which the myth tells us was established by the local hero Erichthonios. This is how it works. Hoplites with chariot and charioteer take part in the race. During the race the hoplite has to dismount and mount the chariot again while the chariot continues its course. Twelve chariots are shown on the north frieze. Some are standing still, others are depicted racing with the charioteer and the hoplite, who is sometimes shown at the precise moment of mounting or dismounting (apobatein = to dismount, from which comes the term apobates).

This is followed by the sacrificial procession. The animals to be sacrificed, four bulls and four rams, are being driven by their attendants. Taking part as well are the thallophoroi, men carrying olive branches, musicians, hydriaphoroi carrying jars of water and skaphephoroi, those who carry the offering trays.

The other section of the procession runs along the south side. Here the flow of the procession changes!

It begins with the marshall who supervises the games. Here too is a file of sixty horsemen. These can be divided into ten groups of six horsemen according to their garb. The horsemen taking part in the procession are grouped by tribe (phyle), following the political organisation of the Athenian state into ten tribes. The procession of chariots follows; ten are shown here. On the next blocks the sacrificial procession is depicted. The sacrificial animals shown are ten bulls and they are accompanied by their drivers. Here too they are followed by tray-bearers, musicians and men with olive branches.

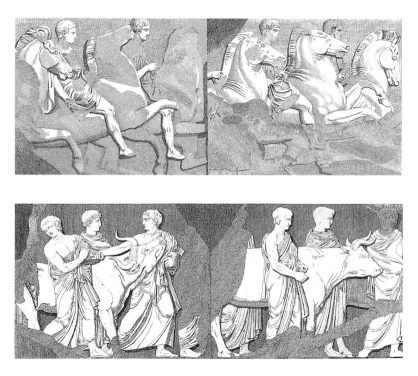

J. Stuart, N. Revett. Restored drawing of sections of the south frieze of the Parthenon, 1751-1753, op. cit.

The sacrificial procession continues on the east end where the two files of the procession meet over the entrance to the temple. The east frieze is the most sacred and this is why no animals are shown here. It is only here, moreover, that women are taking part in the ceremony. At the head of each file, moving toward the centre, women bring the ceremonial vessels for the sacrifice, jugs (oinochoes) and shallow bowls with an omphalos in the centre (phiales) for offering libations, incense burners (thymiateria) and cups (kylikes).

The offering of the peplos (robe) is depicted at the centre above the entrance to the temple. This is the ultimate act, the focal point of the Panathenaic ceremony. Five figures are shown participating in the scene. A priest and a boy hold the peplos. A priestess turns towards two smaller female figures. Seated to left and right are the gods and goddesses. They turn their backs on the sacred scene of the peplos. I myself, Iris, am there too, standing behind Hera.

Between the deities and the procession are the eponymous heroes of Attica, four to the left and six to the right. These are the mythical ancestors of the Athenians, who gave their names to the tribes, that is to the administrative subdivisions of the Athenian state.

So here I end my tour. I have shown you the most wonderful building of the ancient world, just as it was finished by its creators. A building considered by the Athenians to be not only a brilliant dedication to the goddess who protects their city, but a pioneering work of art, both architecture and sculpture, in the framework of their cultural hegemony; it was this cultural phenomenon that lay behind Perikles' conviction that Athens was the school of all Hellas!

J. Stuart, N. Revett. Restored drawing of sections of the east frieze of the Parthenon, 1751-1753, op. cit.

$\mathcal{U}$p to now you have had the privilege of seeing the Parthenon with your imagination, just as it was when it was dedicated in antiquity.

Yet from that time, some twenty-five centuries have come and gone. The temple has seen many vicissitudes and lost forever are many of its parts. The ancient religion has been abandoned, the beautiful myths forgotten. I have ceased to have a place in religion and I can no longer, as a goddess, inspire the artists in their work. I have lost the ability to show you figures that do not now exist and I can no longer give answers to problems that archaeological scholarship has not yet decoded.

So, in this new set of circumstances, we shall continue, we two, our peregrinations. We shall go and look at what is left of the temple and its sculpture; but first let us see what the temple has gone through in all the time that has passed since those far-off days.

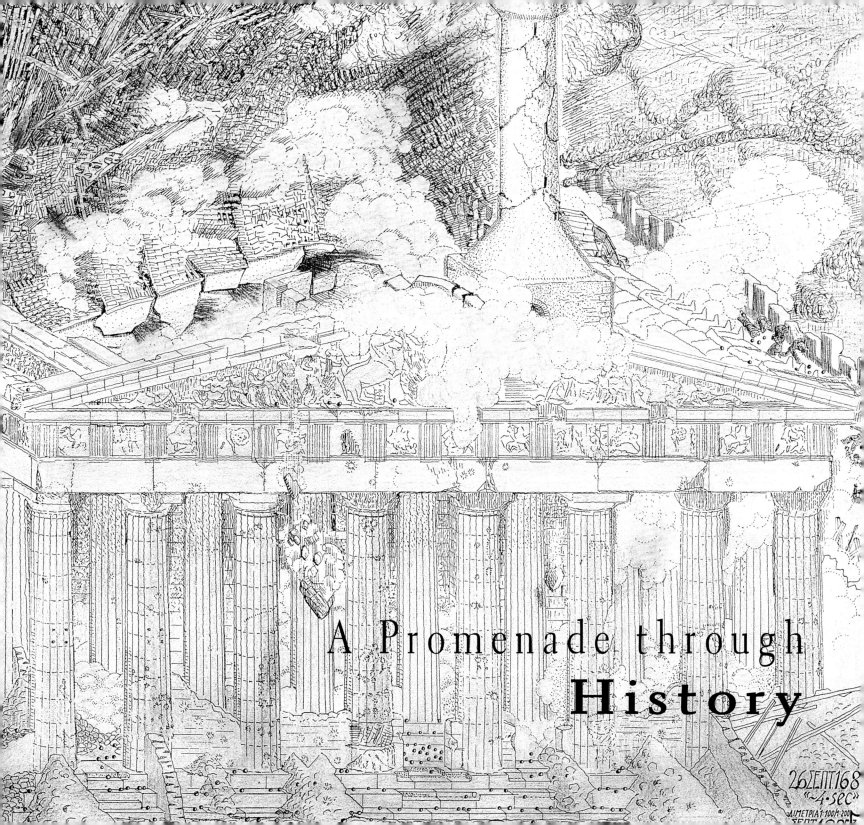

A Promenade through
History

Above: The Parthenon under construction. Drawing by M. Korres.

Previous page: The explosion of the Parthenon on 26 September 1687.
Detail. Dimetrical restoration, drawing by M. Korres.

The Parthenon was built between 447 and 432 B.C. For 700 years the building stood intact. Only the chryselephantine (gold and ivory) statue of Athena Parthenos appears to have been destroyed shortly before 160 B.C. and replaced by another, smaller statue, perhaps of marble.

The first serious catastrophe of the temple occurred much later, probably in A.D. 267 and it was caused by an inflagration. The original roof was destroyed at that time, together with all the interior colonnade and the marble ceilings of the exterior colonnade or peristyle. Seriously damaged were the columns of the hexastyle porches and the cella walls inside. The repair, which goes back to the time of Julian the Apostate, some hundred years later, was carried out with the means and methods of those days and it lacked the quality and the precision of the original work. The sculptured parts, however, appear not to have suffered serious damage at that time.

The interior of the Parthenon just after the fire of A.D. 267, drawing by M. Korres.

By the late 5th or early 6th century, Christianity had taken hold in Greece and the Parthenon was converted into a large church. There is no direct historical information. It is almost certain, however, that this is when the first significant changes were made in the temple, especially to its sculptured decoration: the building was consecrated as a church with the forming of the semi-circular apse of the sanctuary in the pronaos. The main entrance was now from the west through the separate rectangular room, which from then on was used as a narthex, while a door was opened between the two rooms of the cella. Six blocks of the frieze were removed from the long sides in order to open a corresponding number of windows. Part of the east wall of the cella was removed and rebuilt to take in the sanctuary apse.

The new ideas about art during Early Christian times and the strong reaction to the old religion, considered by many to be idolatrous, brought about the destruction of many of those works of art which represented the old divinities or were connected with Greek mythology. The phenomenon was a general one throughout the empire, and the monuments of Athens were no exception. The removal and destruction of the larger statues in the middle of the east pediment and the hacking off of the metopes of the east, west and part of the north sides of the temple, so that the themes represented would not be understood, are dated to the 5th and 6th centuries, although there is no specific information on the subject. It is perhaps not by chance that the last metope of the north side at the west, today in situ, was not cut off; for it is in a way reminiscent of the Annunciation of the Virgin.

The fanaticism of people uneducated in art or history together with the new conditions of an autocratic state led to this frightful destruction. No doubt at that time large metal crosses were set up in the central axis of the pediments, just as stated in the relevant decrees for the consecration of ancient temples.

The Parthenon as a church, east side. Restored drawing by M. Korres.

After this ultimate departure from the beliefs of the ancient world, the centuries rolled on without significant changes. The Parthenon became the church of The Panaghia Atheniotissa (Holy Virgin of Athens), the largest of the city. We know that after the year 1000 it held attraction as a centre of pilgrimage and that it gradually began again to arouse a certain wonder because of its beauty. The pilgrimage of the emperor Basil II in 1018 and the speeches of an educated metropolitan, Michael Choniates at the end of the 12th century, are good examples.

The changes made to the building were few and they were clearly reversible. The same is true of the additions made after 1205 when the Acropolis passed into the hands of the Franks of the 4th Crusade and the Parthenon became a church of the Latin creed. So too later, after 1460, when the Ottoman Turks took Athens and transformed the great temple into a Moslem precinct. In both cases, the changes demanded by the new liturgies were not really serious in terms of the architecture and sculpture of the monument.

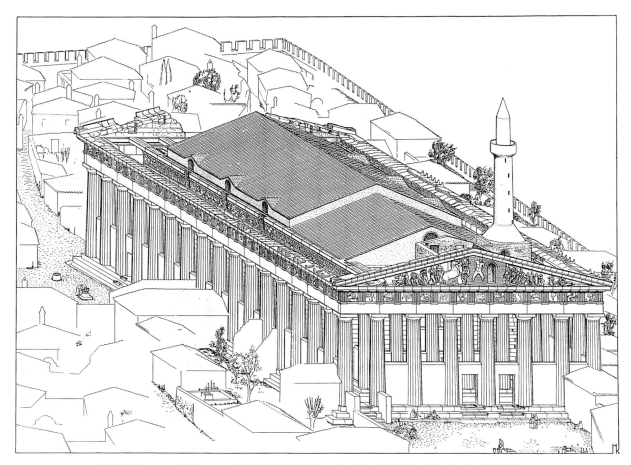

The Parthenon as an Ottoman precinct during the 17th century. Dimetrical restoration, drawing by M. Korres.

47

Thus another 120 years went by. The temple was utilised clumsily, but it was not in any way humbled. In the meantime, new ideas about education, art and life held sway in Europe, the ideas of the Renaissance. The Turkish occupation held Greece outside these new perceptions, an important and determining factor of which was a turn toward the spirit and art of Antiquity. There began to be a lively interest in the monuments that were preserved in Italy and, later, in the originals themselves that were in isolated Greece.

All this is indirectly related to our monument, the Parthenon, which passively was being preserved as an Ottoman mosque. Then, in ever greater numbers, the first Europeans to study the building began to arrive. They left us descriptions, drawings and accounts of their travels. Of singular importance for the study of the sculpture was the visit to Athens of the French ambassador to Constantinople, Charles-Franois Olier, Marquis de Nointel. He arrived with a large following in 1674. Among them was a young artist, probably Jacques Carrey, who made trustworthy drawings of most of the sculptures of the temple which were visible at that time. These drawings are exceedingly valuable because the great destruction occurred thirteen years afterwards.

Parthenon south metopes 17-20. Drawing by J. Carrey 1674, in T. Bowie - D. Thimme,
The Carrey Drawings of the Parthenon Sculptures, London 1971.

Visit to Athens in 1674 of the French ambassador to Constantinople.
View of the city from the northeast. Detail. Oil painting, J. Carrey, Athens, National Gallery.

The war between Venice and the Ottoman empire had begun. The mercenary army of Venice under the command of Francesco Morosini disembarked in Peiraeus and with powerful artillery they bombarded the besieged Turks in the Acropolis. The Turks had stored the powder for their artillery in the Parthenon. Thus, on the evening of the 26th of September 1687, there occurred one of the worst of all the destructions in the history of Greek culture: a frightful explosion that in seconds only turned the temple into ruins, throwing down three of the four cella walls, practically all of the hexastyle colonnade of the pronaos, six columns on the south side and eight along the north. Of the roof, nothing remained. This destruction was followed by a tremendous fire. The monument had suffered a frightful blow.

The Venetians abandonned the Acropolis during the spring of 1688. The Turks re-established themselves and, within the Parthenon, built a small mosque oriented toward Mecca. The way was now wide open for plunder and theft.

The explosion of the Parthenon on 26 September 1687. Dimetrical restoration by M. Korres.

To begin with, the Venetians wanted to take home some statues as souvenirs of their victory, since the Acropolis Fortress had been surrendered to them after the explosion. Thus, aided by implements and crew from their ships, they tried to take down the horses of the chariots of Athena and Poseidon from the west pediment. They failed; the statues crashed to the ground and were shattered into pieces.

Then came the Turks who for more than a century used the ruined Parthenon as a marble quarry for building material and for making lime.

And in the end, the collectors of antiquities came from Europe.

By the end of the 18th century, Count Choiseul-Goufier, the French ambassador to Constantinople, had already obtained a metope and a block from the east frieze with a representation of six maidens and two marshalls. These he sent to France. He was assisted by the French consul in Athens, L. S. Fauvel, who had arranged his own personal collection of antiquities in his house. Today Choiseul-Goufier's two sculptures are exhibited in the Louvre, in the gallery that has taken its name from the Parthenon.

The interest of the Europeans in the monuments of classical antiquity was at its height during the second half of the 18th century. Classicism held sway in architecture and in art, while at the same time travels to the East were becoming easier. Many Englishmen, Frenchmen and Germans of means imitated the aristocrats of Italy and the Popes in acquiring antiquities, particularly vases and statues, disposing the money, knowledge and respect given them by their social position. Up to the Greek revolution of 1821, this mania for acquiring antiquities increased unabated. The result was that many archaeological sites were plundered, in Greece and in Asia Minor too.

L. S. Fauvel in his house. Drawing by Louis Dupré in Voyage à Athènes et Constantinople, Paris, 1825, Athens, Gennadeios Library.

At the very peak of this frenzy came the looting of the Acropolis sculpture by a Scot, Thomas Bruce, the seventh earl of Elgin and eleventh of Kincardine. In 1799 Lord Elgin was appointed as ambassador of his Britannic majesty to the Sublime Porte of Selim III in Constantinople. This was a position which, with the concurrence of the Napoleonic Wars, made him very powerful indeed. Moreover, the Ottoman Empire was in decline.

The facts of the well organised and funded business of looting sculpture from Athens, still under Turkish domination, are well known. Elgin's initial purpose is not entirely clear. Did he want to copy, to make casts of the sculptures or only to take «samples»? Be that as it may, he made certain that he had a «firman», an edict of the sultan, which, with great lack of clarity, gave him permission to work in the Athenian Acropolis, to make excavations, to copy, to make casts of the sculptures and so on. Through his agent, a competent Neapolitan artist, Giovanni Battistta Lusieri, a group of workmen was organised and, having successfully persuaded the Ottoman authorities, the task of removing the sculptures and preparing them for export was begun. Unfortunately their removal was not always a simple matter. A number of geison blocks were thrown to the ground in order to remove the metopes, the relief blocks of the frieze were sawed off along the back in order to reduce their weight for shipping. A Doric column capital was sawed in two for the same purpose.

The Parthenon with the scaffolding for removing the sculpture. Drawing by Sir William Gell, 1801, London, British Museum.

Lord Elgin himself came to Athens during the summer of 1802, when the campaign was already under way. This is when he came up with the idea that the sculpture was in danger and should be removed in order to save it. Work continued and, finally, after various adventures, whatever it had been possible to remove from the Parthenon arrived in London: eighteen pedimental statues, fifteen metopes, together with fifty blocks and two fragments of the frieze that had covered a length of about seventy-five meters. Among the antiquities carried off by Elgin were many others from the Erechtheion, the Thrasyllos monument and even from the Daphni monastery and from Delos.

The Parthenon from the northwest. Oil painting, G. B. Lusieri, 1802, Athens, Benaki Museum.

This activity was soon followed by a storm of protest from all quarters, especially from England, the most authoritative being that of Lord Byron, who a few years later gave his life for the Greek Revolution. Lord Elgin himself was held prisoner for a time in France. Later, financially destroyed, he returned to England. The Elgin collection was sold in 1816 to the British Government, which subsequently offered it to the British Museum. There it was presented in a temporary exhibition between 1817 and 1831.

Shortly before World War II, a new large gallery was built, known as the Duveen Gallery, in which the Parthenon sculpture has been exhibited until today.

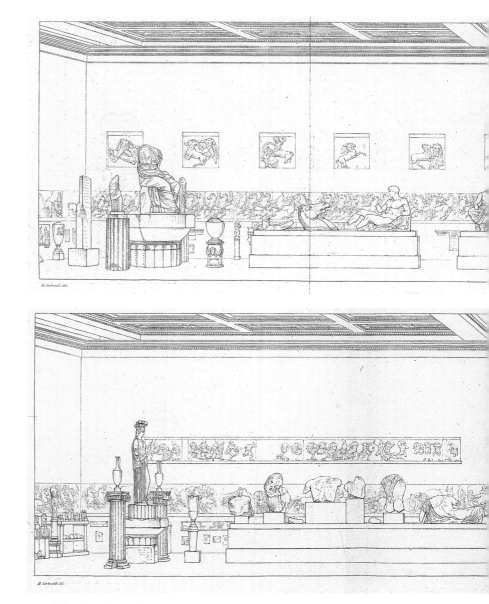

Views of the Elgin gallery in the British Museum. In H. Corbould, description of the Collection of Ancient Marbles in the British Museum, part VII, London 1835, S. Stavrides collection.

Battle and first siege of Athens in 1821-1822. «Thoughts» of Ioannis Makriyannis 1836, work of Panayiotis Zographos, Athens, National Historical Museum.

Siege of Athens in 1827. «Thoughts» of Ioannis Makriyannis 1836, work of Panayiotis Zographos, copy by Demetrios Zographos, Athens, Gennadeios Library.

The years that followed the plundering of the sculpture saw the Greek Revolution. The Acropolis assumed great strategic value as a fortress. It was now at the very centre of military operations and the monuments suffered further damage as a result. Defensive manoeuvres were organised for the most part along the west and south sides, behind a wall, known as the Serpetzé, which incorporated the tall façade of the Odeion of Herodes Attikos. The Acropolis was twice besieged during the course of the struggle, first by the Greeks (1821-1822), and then by the Turks under Kioutachi Pasha (1827). General Makriyannis, who was an eye-witness of both sieges, gives us much relevant information. Under his direction, a popular artist, named Panayiotis Zographos, later drew twenty-four pictures of battle scenes; two of these depict the two sieges most expressively and with large descriptive titles by Makriyannis.

From 1835 on, the Acropolis monuments were for the first time under the supervision of scholars. Cleaning, excavations and, later on, anastelosis (restoration) would be carried out.

A considerable number of the sculptural decoration of the great temple escaped the ravages of Elgin, since they were buried beneath the ruins of various additions, and it was possible to excavate them, carry out their conservation and later exhibit them in the Acropolis Museum, where we may see them today.

Consolidation and anastelosis has revived the building itself to its present state. A number of architectural members have been set again in place in an effort to give the damaged building some structural and formal continuity and to make it more readily understood by those who come to see it. The most extensive anastelosis programmes were carried out between 1898 and 1933. This is known as the Balanos programme and it included the anastelosis of eight columns of the north colonnade together with the entablature and five columns on the south side.

The Parthenon from the northwest. Daguerreotype, P. G. Joly de Lotbiniére, 1839, Athena, Benaki Museum, Geroyannis-Petmezas collection.

*The eastern end of the north side of the Parthenon around 1913.
Photo Fr. Boissonas. In Le Parthenon, l'histoire, l'architecture et la sculpture, Paris, 1914.*

With the passage of some forty years, it was evident that new work was needed, for two reasons: first, the metal pieces that had been inserted in the Balanos anastelosis had rusted out and, second, because of atmospheric pollution. In 1975, the interdisciplinary Committee for the Preservation of the Acropolis Monuments was formed. This established the technical office of the Acropolis and it planned the restoration of the monuments, initiating new research on an international scale and new applications concerning the anastelosis of ancient monuments.

Unfortunately, atmospheric pollution had directly affected the few sculptures that still remained on the Parthenon. It was therefore determined that in order to save them from the surface deterioration

caused by pollution, they would have to be removed and kept in a closed area, that is a museum, and replaced by exact copies. Thus, over the last twenty years, the group of Kekrops and his daughter and the statue of the nymph Kallirrhoe have been removed from the west pediment from the east, the heads of the Horses of Selene were removed. Finally, in 1994, the Ionic frieze of the west end, over twenty meters in length, was taken down and placed in the Museum as an ultimate solution to its preservation.

The method followed for the intervention in every section of the temple has been: careful documentation and analysis of the evidence, removal of the parts, conservation, their restoration and re-setting. The east side shows such a programme in completion. From the beginning of the work a crane was placed in the Parthenon cella. Some 160 members of the monument, weighing a total of 350 tons, have been removed, undergone conservation and been set again in place on the monument. The corner sima with the lion head and the metopes of the east side that had been damaged by hacking have been taken to the Museum. They have been replaced on the monument by exact copies made of artificial stone.

The vicissitudes of its long life have left their mark forever on the marble of the great temple and this helps us in studying its course through time. Traces of ancient tools and later tools as well, marks of fire, traces of mediaeval inscriptions, remains of the wall paintings of the church, the marks of Morosini's bombardment, of the gouging out of lead for bullets, as well as alveoral decay and erosion caused by atmospheric pollution; all these are now elements of history.

The return of the sculpture of Lord Elgin's collection to Athens has been a hope of the Greeks ever since the establishment of the Greek state. The request has been supported by many people of culture from all over the world and from England too, because they believe that these inestimable works of ancient art are the heritage of the Greek people and that they should be together with what has been saved in Athens.

The most important effort toward achieving this was initiated by the unforgetable Melina Merkouri in 1984 when she was Minister of Culture. Her appeal met response throughout the world. It mobilised well-known people in Greece and England and created a positive outlook for the return of the sculpture. It is hoped that this can be achieved in the not too distant future. The Melina Merkouri Foundation was established in Athens after her death and continues her efforts. The request is closely connected with the planned construction of a new Museum below the Sacred Rock, which will be able to accommodate all of the sculptured decoration of the temple.

The Parthenon sculpture has been much admired and many books and articles have been written about it. All the casts of the Parthenon sculpture are today on exhibition in the Museum of Antiquities in Basel, Switzerland, and in the Centre for Acropolis Studies in Athens.

*N*ow that we have made ourselves familiar with the history of the Parthenon, it is time to return to the reality of the present day, to your own time, to see the monument as it is right now. Unseen, I shall still walk beside you and together we shall look at whatever has survived, just as it appears to those who could not travel with me into antiquity. Many members of the temple have disappeared forever. Some of the sculpture hardly recalls what we saw on our brief walk into the past. Many questions can no longer be answered. No one today can really know precisely how the temple looked 2,500 years ago.

A Promenade on the
Acropolis

Let us climb the Acropolis and go through the Propylaia. In front of us stands the Parthenon, the great temple of Athena. Some 2500 years have passed since it was built, but, from this point at least, from its northwest side, it appears at first glance to be practically intact. It has not lost its grandeur or the unique fascination of its size and the harmony of proportion that belies its mass.

Yet if we approach the Parthenon more closely, we see that it is an empty shell, a ruin without a roof, with large parts of the cella and colonnades destroyed and damage in many places to the columns, the entablature and the walls. Worst of all, the building is without the fine sculpture that embellished it.

Of its once rich sculptural decoration, only a few pieces now remain in situ. Many have been lost forever, others have been irreparably altered or are preserved only in fragments. Many others are in museums where they are displayed as isolated sculptural works, homeless representatives of classical Greek art.

General view of the Parthenon from the northwest.

Right page: View of the south colonnade and the cella wall of the Parthenon from the east.

Previous page: East frieze, block VI, detail.

66

Part of the north side of the Parthenon.

View of the first south metope.

View of the last north metope.

What remains on the building itself today of the sculptural decoration? The hammer-hacked metopes of the west, a few of those on the north side, and the two west corner metopes of the long sides. These two are among the most beautiful of those we know. The one on the south side shows a Centaur grasping the throat of a Lapith, while he prepares to strike him with his outstretched right hand. On the other, already discussed, are two female figures, probably goddesses, one upright and the other sitting upon a rock; they wear garments with rich folds.

The educational value of these two pieces of sculpture, still in place upon the temple, is obvious. Also on the temple, we note quite a few copies, made during recent years to replace the original works that have been removed to the Museum. Let us go and have a look at the originals.

The Acropolis Museum was built between 1865 and 1874 according to the plans of the architect Panaghis Kalkos, specifically to house the Acropolis antiquities. Today it has four fairly large galleries and five smaller ones. Here we can see the best of the temple sculpture that has remained on the Acropolis.

The Acropolis Museum.

Come and see the pediments

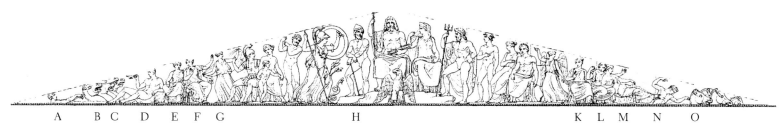

A   B C D E F G   H   K L M N O

Restored drawing of the east pediment in H. Corbould, description of the Collection of Ancient Marbles in the British Museum, part VI, London 1830, S. Stavridis collection.

This female figure wearing a peplos, leaning forward and downward comes from the **east pediment.** Her peplos is belted at the waist and crossed over at the breast. Bronze decorations had been applied to the knot of her belt and on her shoulders. She is the personification of **Selene** who was driving her chariot down into the sea in the righthand corner of the pedimental scene. Three of the four heads of the chariot team are in the Museum. The forth and most beautiful of the horseheads was carried off.

East pediment, figure N, Selene (Acrop. 881).

70

Fragment of a head, Hera (Acrop. 2381).

The over life-sized female statue likewise belongs to the east pediment. She is preserved in two fragments, both in poor condition. This is **Hera** who stood next to Zeus. She wears a long peplos, belted high. Despite its worn condition, the statue, known also as the Wegner peplophoros, is distinguished by its superb quality. Attributed to this same statue is a head fragment with three rows of holes in the hair which once supported a gilded crown.

Look at this. It is the upper part of a stalwart male torso turning toward the right. It is **Hephaistos** who, as you know, played an important part in the scene of the birth of Athena. It is fairly well preserved.

Fragments of the Wegner Peplophoros, Hera (Acrop. 6711 and 879)

East pediment, figure H, Hephaistos (Acrop. 880).

Restored drawing of the west pediment. In H. Corbould, description of the Collection of Ancient Marbles in the British Museum, part VI, London 1830, S. Stavridis collection.

None of the figures from the **west pediment** were preserved completely, although we know far more about this pediment through Carrey's drawings.

The upper part of **Poseidon's** torso is preserved in two parts: the front is in the Acropolis, the back in London. Even though the arms are missing the figure is striking with its great size and naturalistic beauty. His left leg was bent while with his right hand he raised the trident.

Of the gigantic figure of **Athena** we have only part of the neck and back of the head; the face has been destroyed. She wore a helmet and had various attachments, such as an earring on her right ear.

West pediment, figure M, Poseidon (Acrop. 885).

From the left angle of the west pediment comes this group of **Kekrops** and his daughter, **Pandrossos.** Kekrops wearing a himation, is sitting on the ground resting himself on one hand, and his daughter wearing chiton and himation, kneeling, embraces him around his shoulder. Both these statues, cut from the same block of marble, are headless now and their front surfaces show marked erosion from atmospheric pollution. Yet some details of anatomy and carving of the drapery on the back and sides of the group still show their fine classical quality. The group included also a snake, which has however been taken. It was coiled at the feet of Kekrops, showing clearly that he is indeed the mythical first king of the city.

West pediment, group B-C, Kekrops and Pandrossos (Acrop. 14935).

*Fragment of a horse head
(Acrop. 882).*

Two broken heads and a leg are all that remain of the horses of the chariots to the left and right of the central axis of the pediment, with some other small fragments kept in the Museum storerooms.

*Fragment of a horse head
(Acrop. 884).*

*West pediment,
figure U (Acrop. 1363).*

In the Museum we can also see four very important statues from the right wing of the pediment.

The first is a female figure seated on a rock wearing a chiton and himation. Missing are the upper part of the body and the left knee.

Acrop. 888.

To her right, also on a rock, sat another woman wearing peplos and h i m a t i o n . Unfortunately only a fragment of the statue, from the

Then comes the personification of the Attic river, **Ilissos,** who is depicted kneeling, virtually nude, with a himation showing only at the back of the torso. Here too, unfortunately, the head is missing, as are the legs and arms. Surface erosion is evident all over. His right arm may have been raised. This statue is ranked among the masterpieces that adorned the monument.

West pediment, figure V, Ilissos (Acrop. 887).

Still further to the right we see yet another female figure, stretched out. This represents a personification of the spring **Kallirrhoe.** Although it was protected by the pedimental geison, the work has to a great extent been destroyed. The upper part is missing for its entire length. The rich folds of the drapery show the real ability of the classical sculptor who created this work.

West pediment, figure W, Kallirrhoe (Acrop. 14936).

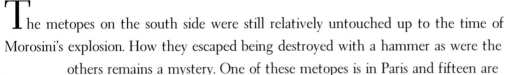

Come and see the metopes

Of the ninety-two metopes that once decorated the Parthenon, twenty-three are still in place. Their surfaces are much destroyed except for the two we have already seen. It is difficult indeed to recognise the themes on some of these hammer-hacked metopes. Along the east front the metopes have already been replaced by copies and removed to the Museum.

Centaur head
(Acrop. 720).

The metopes on the south side were still relatively untouched up to the time of Morosini's explosion. How they escaped being destroyed with a hammer as were the others remains a mystery. One of these metopes is in Paris and fifteen are in the British Museum. The others were shattered. It was possible to put together No. 12, from large fragments. This we see now in the Museum. It shows a Centaur coming from the right and seizing a Lapith woman. The heads are missing from both figures, but, even so, the details are admirable.

Many other small fragments of the south metopes including three well preserved heads, of a Lapith, a Lapith woman and a Centaur, are in the Acropolis Museum, some on exhibition, some in the storerooms. Continuing research by archaeologists is producing more joins and even unknown metopes have been completed.

Head of Lapith woman
(Acrop. 1309).

South metope 12
(Acrop. 705).

Head of Lapith
(Acrop. 6511).

The frieze is the best preserved of all the sculptural elements of the temple. We have already discussed the subject, the Panathenaic procession, and its general arrangement. In the Acropolis Museum we can admire and study detached pieces, large and small, as independent works of art.

In addition to the west frieze, which survived in situ virtually intact and was removed to the Acropolis Museum for protection in a closed area, we can see significant sections from all four sides, which had been removed or had fallen from their places and had luckily escaped the pillaging.

Come and see the frieze

The heavy transverse beams of the west colonnade and the immovable overlying blocks, the thranoi (crowning blocks over the frieze) prevented Elgin's men from removing the **west frieze,** with the exception of the last two blocks at the north. Look at the parade of horsemen. Some are talking together, one is harnessing his horse, others are trying to rein in their horses, some are preparing to mount and two are adjusting their sandals. The horse of one of the heralds is in a pose that is unique on the frieze; so natural is the movement, one might almost call it anti-monumental. It bends its head to rub it against its leg.

Section of the west frieze before its removal from the monument. Blocks VII, VIII, IX are shown, photo L. Bouras, Photographic Archive, Benaki Museum.

A relief in the middle of the frieze is particularly impressive with the splendid understanding and rendition of the figure of a rider who is trying to rein in his bolting horse. His movement is free, his drapery billows out behind him and the animal's head is reminiscent of the horsehead in the group of Selene's chariot in the east pediment. Many have suggested that this extraordinary relief is by the hand of Pheidias himself.

The relief of the west side in essence shows the preparation for the procession. Special care has been taken to impart variety and liveliness to the whole

West frieze, block XII, photo L. Bouras, Photographic Archive, Benaki Museum.

West frieze, block VIII, photo L. Bouras,
Photographic Archive, Benaki Museum.

West frieze, block VI. Detail. Photo L. Bouras,
Photographic Archive, Benaki Museum.

The procession on the **north side** moves from right to left.

Let us have a better look at the horses!

They are all shown in profile. They have delicate limbs and the rendition of head, eyes and muzzle, as also of mane and tail, gives to most of them an individual character. Look how many horses you can see on the same block! Just count their legs.

North frieze, block XXXVI (A.M. XXXI).

The figures have been very skillfully arranged so that neither those on foot nor those mounting are taller than the horses. They all fit easily into the framework of the frieze.

Now let us look at the horsemen. Some look straight ahead, others turn their heads to look downwards. The young riders are beardless and wear short chitons or are shown nude. You can make out the little holes that were for the insertion of metal attachments. Despite the great damage suffered by these last reliefs, some of the faces have survived, such as that of a young marshall who turns back to make a signal, a figure of truly singular beauty and charm.

North frieze, block XXXIV (A.M. XXIX).

Preserved on a large fragment is one of the most beautiful reliefs of the temple. It depicts a nude marshall who, with a lively movement backwards, gives a signal to restrain some chariot horses that have broken into a gallop. Let's have a closer look at the chariot: it had two wheels which supported the biga, that is the body of the chariot. You can make out the charioteer and also the apobates who is shown at the exact moment of leaping onto the moving chariot. They are both holding onto the rail. The horses are yoked to the chariot by means of a strong shaft which was attached to the axis of the wheels.

North frieze, block XXIII (A.M. XVII).

82

North frieze, block XI.

North frieze, block XXVII (A.M. XXII).

The race of the apobates is shown on other sections as well, some moving, some standing. The hoplites wear short chitons, plumed helmets, and they carry heavy round shields.

Now notice that the procession on the **south side** moves from left to right. Here, apart from various fragments, only two blocks have survived in reasonably good condition. They show horsemen riding at a gallop.

South frieze, block XVI.

South frieze, block XVII.

The procession of the sacrifice on the north side can be seen practically in its entirety in the Acropolis Museum. Two relatively well preserved blocks show youths leading bulls and rams destined for sacrifice.

North frieze, block II.

The horizontal axes formed by the bodies of the bulls and the vertical lines of the men in the procession, especially the youth whose entire body is covered by his himation, make the composition very interesting. The bull who signals his refusal to follow the procession by a swing of his head and the movement of his legs, shows in relief a completely new perception of artistic freedom.

North frieze, block IV.

Four skaphephoroi, men bringing trays with offerings, followed the rams. One of these, from the south side, is in the Acropolis Museum.

Next, on a virtually undamaged block, three hydria bearers are depicted. These are youths carrying the heavy jars full of water necessary for the sacrifice. They wear himations. Behind them is a forth, perhaps nude, who has put down his hydria, to rest for a moment. Notice the slight differences in the poses of the water bearers –in the turn of the head, the hands, the drapery folds– which give variety to the whole and proclaim as well the individuality of each.

Acrop. 1140, tray bearer.

North frieze, block VI, water-jar bearers.

Depicted on the blocks that follow are musicians with auloi, the double pipes (the arms of a player can be seen on the preceding block) and kitharas. The sound-box and arms of the kithara are preserved. These blocks are in very poor condition as is also the next one with the old men bearing olive branches (thallophoroi) and following in the procession. The next block, with the same theme, is in far better condition, with damage only to the faces of the thallophoroi. The aged men, sixteen in number, held olive branches (thalloi or olive shoots) which were painted on the ground of the block rather than being shown in relief.

North frieze, block VIII, musicians.

North frieze, block X, olive-branch bearers.

Two sections of the main, the **eastern side** of the frieze, are shown here. The first from the left end, is made up of fragments and shows girls holding shallow bowls (phialai) and taking part in the procession.

East frieze, block II.

East frieze, block VI. Detail.

The second is preserved in excellent condition. It includes three of the company of deities to which, as you know, the Panathenaic procession leads. Depicted here is Poseidon holding his trident, Apollo crowned and holding a laurel branch and Artemis with her bow. Turned towards the right, they are sitting on simple stools –the diphros. They radiate the Olympian felicity that classical art gave the gods. Artemis' chiton is impressive with its rich folds revealing the lines of her body. By good fortune, the heads of all three figures are preserved together with their features. It is otherwise with Aphrodite who sat just to the right: preserved are only her legs, wrapped in the rich folds of her garment and a small piece of her head. While we know very well, from an old cast, how Eros will have looked –a small boy, nude, leaning against his mother's legs and holding a little parasol– we will not see him in the Museum. For the figure has been lost since the nineteenth century.

Among the fragments we can see here are the head of a girl and part of the figure representing me, Iris. It is said to be one of the most beautiful heads of Greek classical sculpture. The rest of my figure is in London.

Acrop. 1189.

East frieze, block V. Detail.
Acrop. 855.

Youthful figures from the north frieze.
Top row: 1. block XXXIV (A.M. XXIX). 2. block XXXVI (A.M. XXXI). - Bottom row: 1. block IV. 2. block II.

By now I am sure you will have understood the splendid unity of this great work, the frieze. Nothing has been overdone. The gods are on the same level as ordinary mortals and differ little from the citizens taking part in the procession. At the same time, no single mortal is over-emphasised. The poses are natural, all are calm and by their movements they emphasise the meaning of their participation. All express the coherence of Athenian society of the golden age that ordered this work and is represented in it. Indeed, it was well said that this magnificent sculptural work is no less than the expression of Democracy itself, at its best moment in antiquity.

To fill in the picture given by the sculpture of the Parthenon today and to compare it with what we have seen on our promenade into time past, we must make yet another expedition, this time to England, to the British Museum.

A Promenade in the
British Museum

The British Museum was built between 1823 and 1847 according to the plans of Sir Robert Smirke in order to house the various collections that had already accumulated in London. We enter at the south side of that enormous museum, through the big colonnade with tall Ionic columns and a pediment with sculpture, framed by two wings likewise of the Ionic order. This is an example of the classicism that prevailed in English architecture at the time, shortly after the arrival there of the Parthenon sculpture.

The British Museum.

The wing that carries the name of Lord Duveen was built within the museum shortly before World War II. It comprises a long narrow gallery with high ceiling. Around the walls have been placed the fragments of the frieze and the metopes. The pedimental sculpture is displayed on two bases, one at each end of the gallery. Shown in two other smaller rectangular rooms are other architectural members and information about the Acropolis and its monuments.

Come and see the pediments

From the pediments come the most beautiful sculptures of Elgin's collection. The fact that they are exhibited on a base placed at some distance from the wall enables us to have a good look at them and to examine the backs of the figures as well, something that was quite impossible in antiquity. We should remember that these statues were made as a dedication to the goddess, so that the back, even if not visible to the mortals, had to be completed and just as beautiful as the main aspect of the figure.

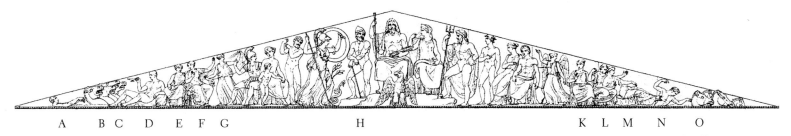

A   B C D   E F G   H   K L M N   O

Restored drawing of the east pediment. In H. Corbould, description of the Collection of Ancient Marbles in the British Museum, part VI, London 1830, S. Stavridis collection.

Previous page: East pediment, group K-L-M, Hestia, Dione and Aphrodite.

East pediment, group A-C, Helios and his chariot.

Helios, the sun, in the left angle of the **east pediment,** rises from the sea. His arms outstretched, he holds the reins of his chariot team. The four horses too are rising from the sea. See the waves which are carved on the marble; they lap the horses' necks.

Beside them we see one of the best known of the statues in the collection: a young man, nude, stretched out on an animal skin. He is identified as the god **Dionysos** who held a kantharos (drinking cup) in his hand, now missing. Some art historians think that the figure was meant to be Herakles and that the hide is the hero's famous lion-skin. This is the only pedimental statue of which the head, though damaged, is preserved. The statue has been much admired for its naturalistic rendering together with its idealistic proportions. Worth noting too is the way one leg projects beyond the boundary of the pediment.

East pediment, figure D, Dionysos.

Next to this we see two female figures cut out of a single block of marble. They are sitting on square blocks and wear peplos and himation, their garments falling in rich folds. Their heads are now missing, but some details, particularly of the drapery, are very well preserved. The couple represents **Demeter** and her daughter, **Persephone.** Demeter is turned toward the middle of the pediment and raises her right arm in lively fashion. She is set at an angle so that this single piece of marble protrudes from the pediment thus breaking the mass. Persephone sits easily beside her looking ahead. Here too the sculptor has shown the harmonious modelling of the body beneath the folds of the garment with the same naturalness and extraordinary skill.

East pediment, group E-F,
Persephone and Demeter.

Notice the strong connection between body and drapery, how the folds are gathered and fall free, how the knee is shown beneath the drapery. Look how tenderly the daughter rests against her mother. Finally, see how they form a triangle together with Dionysos, how naturally they are made to fit into the scheme of the pediment.

The figure of **Artemis** is next in this composition. Upright, she rushes to the left, while turning her head toward the centre. She wears a long peplos and a himation which billows out behind her like a sail. The folds of her drapery are simpler still than those we have seen on the other statues. The himation was cut from the same block of marble as the body. Her entire leg projects from the opening of her garment, which is for this reason called a phainomeris (a garment exposing the limbs).

East pediment, figure G, Artemis.

From the right hand angle of the east pediment come another three female figures. The first represents **Hestia,** who sits and looks frontally. She wears a light chiton and heavier himation.

Next are two female figures again cut from a single block of marble. They are **Dione** and her daughter **Aphrodite.** You can see that the group, with Aphrodite in her mother's arms, has a triangular composition so that it fits into the pedimental wedge. Here too, the heads and arms are missing. Yet the statues are preserved in good condition and the Pentelic marble shows its natural translucence and the patina given by time. On all three statues the skillfully cut folds of the drapery model the forms of the body beneath the thin chiton and hang down to cover the rock with a himation on which the goddess of beauty reclines. Look how the drapery is gathered between the legs, how it encircles the breast, leaving the shoulder exposed.

East pediment, group K-L-M, Hestia, Dione and Aphrodite.

Further to the right is the head of a **horse** from **Selene's** team. This is an extraordinarily lively rendition, despite the schematisation intended for the viewer at a distance.

Worth noting is the freedom of the composition, how the head of the lovely creature rises above the cymatia (moulding) of the horizontal geison and protrudes at an angle. This is one of the best known works exhibited in the British Museum. A series of small holes shows that its mane was metal and attached. A copy has now been placed in the pediment of the temple.

East pediment, figure O,
head of one of Selene's horses.

Restored drawing of the west pediment. In H. Corbould, description of the Collection of Ancient Marbles in the British Museum, part VI, London 1830, S. Stavridis collection.

From the **west pediment** of the Parthenon come some of the most impressive sculpture in the British Museum.

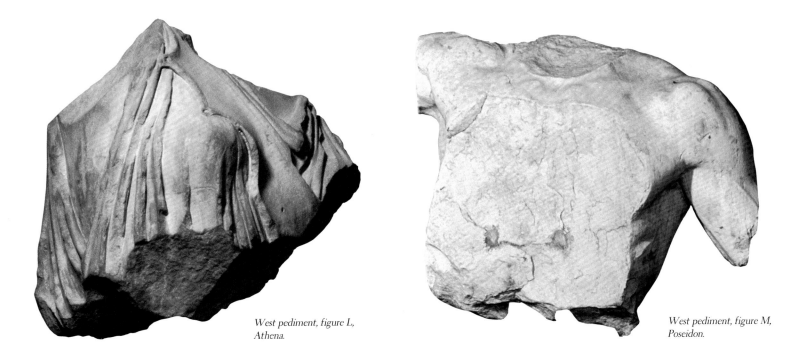

West pediment, figure L, Athena.

West pediment, figure M, Poseidon.

Of the central figures of the pediment, the back of the torso of **Poseidon** (the front is in the Acropolis Museum) and part of the body of **Athena** are preserved. Look at Athena. The statue was colossal, with an original height of around 3,30 meters The aegis was placed obliquely across her breast and it has holes for the attachment of bronze snakes and in the middle a gorgoneion (head of Medusa).

West pediment, figure A,
Kephisos.

From the west angle of the pediment comes a male figure, the personification of one of the rivers of Attica, the **Kephissos.** The figure is reclining, nude –the himation is best seen from the back– and he tries to rise, supporting himself on his left hand. Even though here too the arms and head are missing, the splendid vigour of the male form and faultless rendition of the anatomy are apparent. The flowing of the river and the tumbling of water are suggested by the plasticity of the body.

In the right wing is **Amphitrite,** Poseidon's wife, who drove his chariot. She is clad in a high-belted chiton, without sleeves; little holes are visible for bronze attachments at her waist and jewellery at her neck. Her limbs and head are missing.

West pediment, figure O,
Amphitrite.

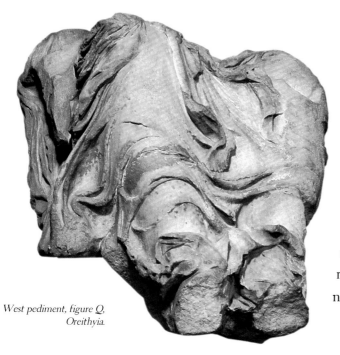

West pediment, figure Q,
Oreithyia.

Next to her is **Oreithyia.** Only the lower part of the statue is preserved. Even though she is shown seated, the splendid swirling folds of her drapery remind us that she was the wife of the north wind, Boreas.

The torso of **Hermes,** unfortunately in very worn condition, stands to the left of the central figures. Here too, the god's garment is visible only from behind. Small holes were for the attachment of some metal shoulder strap, perhaps a sling for a weapon. The left thigh is in Athens. The movement evident in the entire body portrays the messenger of the gods.

West pediment, figure H, Hermes.

106

Laborde head, Paris, Louvre.

I, **Iris,** am shown in the corresponding position in the right wing of the pediment, running toward the centre of the scene. My head and limbs are missing. I am dressed in a light, sleeveless chiton, gathered high at the waist by a bronze belt which was attached. See the fine skill with which the artist has rendered my lively movement, as the wind plays with the light chiton on my body revealing its beauty. The great wings which were attached to my back have by now disappeared. To this, my statue, belonged the most beautiful head, known as the «Laborde head» and now in Paris in the Louvre.

West pediment, figure N, Iris.

Come and see the metopes

All fifteen metopes of the Elgin collection come from the south side of the temple. All show scenes of the Centauromachy and can be studied better from the Carrey drawings, which were made before the damage caused by the explosion of 1687.

South metope, no. 31.

South metope, no. 27.

Let's recall the theme: the Centaurs, guests at the wedding of Peirithoos, King of the Lapiths, got drunk, and tried to make off with the women. This was followed by a battle in which various pieces of palace equipment were used.

On the square of each metope is a scene with two figures, a bearded Centaur and a beardless Lapith. The figures are arranged in all sorts of combinations. One is shown hitting another, one tramples another, the Centaurs rise up, some on their forelegs, some on their hindlegs, while others are shown kneeling. Look how the anatomical details of the nude bodies are emphasised, how some of the faces of the Centaurs resemble masks, look how they grab their opponent by the hair, how they raise their shields in defense, how they skid on a fallen vessel. The composition may well belong to Pheidias, but various workshops surely did the actual carving. In good classical tradition, the faces express humanity and calm. There is no beastliness in the faces of the Centaurs nor do the Lapith faces show fright. On some of the metopes the Lapith wins the fight, on others the Centaur. The battle's outcome is in the balance.

South metope, no. 4.

South metope, no. 28.
Following pages: South metope, no. 2. - South metope, no. 30.

Come and see the frieze

Now we come to the frieze with the Panathenaic procession. The blocks, with scenes in relief, are frequently termed slabs since Elgin's men as a rule sawed off the backs of the frieze blocks in order to reduce their weight for transportation.

West frieze, block II.

Elgin was able to remove only two blocks of the **west frieze**, from the north end. These we see here. The first shows two young horsemen, galloping freely; one is nude with a chlamys and the other wears a short chiton and cuirass. Both men and horses are distinguished by different characteristics. Look at the horses' manes. Notice too the way the body of the nude rider is turned, his head likewise, his hair flying and his chlamys billowing in the wind.

Northwest corner block.

On the other block the corner is preserved complete and we can note that the frieze comprised 117 blocks-architectural members with an average thickness of 65 centimeters, the visible surfaces of which were decorated with figures in relief.

On one side of the corner block a standing marshall is depicted, closely wrapped in his himation.

North frieze, block XLVII (B.M. XLII).

Now take a look at the scene shown on the other side of the corner, the beginning of the **north frieze.** A child is shown fastening the belt of the man standing in front of him, arranging the folds of his short chiton.

113

Let us keep in mind the fact that the procession on the two long sides has each a different course; let's try to see the two units at the same time. On the north side of the frieze, as you will remember, the procession moves from right to left; on the south from left to right. The general arrangement is roughly the same and it is as follows: horses galloping, chariots, and the sacrificial procession with olive branch bearers (thallophoroi), musicians, bearers of vessels and the animals.

If you look at this section, which is better preserved, you will see that the scenes illustrated on the frieze follow one after the other without being restricted by the size of the block into which they have been cut. We must note here that specialists on ancient art disagree about the order of the frieze blocks.

Let us see first of all the horsemen who are riding their horses. Exhibited in London are fourteen blocks from the **south** procession of riders. We can see that they run in ten groups of six each, distinguishable by their different garments. From the north side thirteen blocks are on exhibit. The sixty horsemen here too form ten groups, but they are not equally divided.

North frieze, block XLII (B.M. XXXVII).

North frieze, block XLIII (B.M. XXXVIII).

The axes formed by the heads and bodies of the horses and riders create an impression of movement. Look at the galloping horses, how they move, how they compete with each other. Some are in the air; without a hoof on the ground.

The good preservation of some of the blocks and some of the horses and men is really striking. Here again we see the extraordinary variety, not only of movement (especially the movement of the heads), but also in the gestures, the garments, the footgear and headgear. Frequently repeated is the motive of a horseman turning his head back. See how beautiful they are, in keeping with classical idealism. The severe profiles of the men breathe ethos, spirituality and pride.

South frieze, block X.

South frieze, block XI.

North frieze, block XLIV (B.M. XXXIX).

South frieze, block XIII.

From the group of chariots on the north side come five blocks with significant gaps as well as many fragments. Here we can see the chariot, the wheels, the biga where the charioteer stood to hold the reins and guide it in the race.

North frieze, block XXIV (B.M. XVIII).

At least five chariots have been lost from the south side. Some of these we know from Carrey's drawings. On exhibit are five blocks; there are wide gaps in the scene. On one of these blocks we see a chariot racing with an armed Athenian who turns his head back. With superb skill the sculptor has created a brilliant composition and at the same time, in a relief only five centimeters high, he has managed to render the four horse heads on different planes.

South frieze, block XXXI (B.M. XXX).

North frieze, block XLI (B.M. XXXVI). Detail.

Of interest is the way in which the horsemen rein in their horses with metal reins, now lost. The evidence for reconstruction of these details lies in the little holes for the application of metal and in the various positions of the hands: hands resting, hands clenched, hands that were holding the reins, pulling on them. In addition, hands stroking the horses, hands gesturing to others in the procession or gathering or making fast their hair, all contributing to the tremendous variety of the composition.

South frieze, block XXVI (B.M. XXV). Detail.

North frieze, block XLIV (B.M. XXXIX). Detail.

Top row: *1. North frieze, block XLIII (B.M. XXXVIII). 2. North frieze, block XLII (B.M. XXXVII). 3. North frieze, block XLVII (B.M. XLII). 4. South frieze, block XIII.*

Middle row: 1. North frieze, block XXXVII (B.M. XXXII). 2. North frieze, block XLVII (B.M. XLIII). 3. West frieze, block II. 4. South frieze, block X.

Bottom row: 1. North frieze, block XLIV (B.M. XXXIX). 2. North frieze, block XL (B.M. XXXV). 3. North frieze, block XLI (B.M. XXXVI). 4. South frieze, block X.

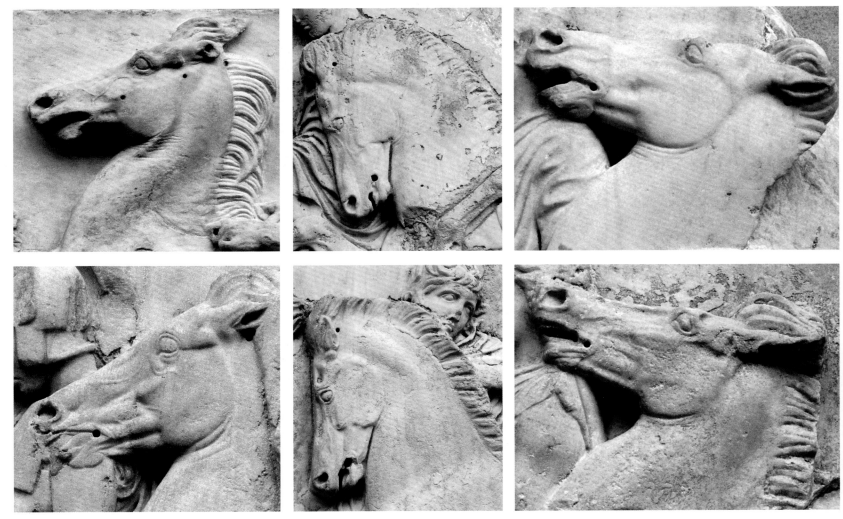

Top row: 1. West frieze, block II. 2. North frieze, block XXXVII (B.M. XXXII). 3. North frieze, block XXXVII (B.M. XXXII).
Bottom row: 1. North frieze, block XLIII (B.M. XXXVIII). 2. North frieze, block XLI (B.M. XXXVI). 3. North frieze, block XL (B.M. XXXV).

Of the group of elderly Athenians following the procession, only a fragment preserving the lower part is on exhibit here. Of the rest of the procession, the exhibition has a single relief of a tray-bearer. Only small fragments remain from the musicians and bearers of vessels, and we do not know with certainty where they belong. London has, by contrast, six fairly well preserved blocks showing youths with long himatia leading bulls for the great sacrifice to the goddess. Here too there is variety: one bull has run amok and is being restrained with difficulty; another tosses his head, while a third bends down with all his strength.

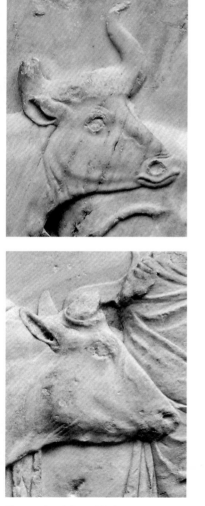

Top: South frieze, block XLVI
*   (B.M. XXXVIII).*
Bottom: South frieze, block XLI.

South frieze, block XLIV (B.M. XL).

East frieze, block III. Detail.

East frieze, block VIII.

The British Museum has the following pieces from the **east end** of the frieze: the rest of the scene of the seated deities, the scene of giving the peplos, two groups one of four and one of six people and, finally, two more groups of girls who approach from the left and right holding the sacred vessels for the ceremonies, incense burners (thymiateria), jugs (oinochoai) and shallow bowls (phialai) for libations.

East frieze, block IV. Detail.

124

The group of deities is divided into two to accomodate the scene of handing over the peplos. The relief is preserved in relatively good condition, except for the faces of the divinities, which had been destroyed on purpose.

Zeus holds a sceptre and his throne has a back and arms which are decorated with little sphinxes. Next to him sits Hera who raises her peplos, turning toward him with a gesture known in ancient art and signifying married couples. I myself, Iris, stand behind her, my head missing from the block, but preserved in Athens. To the left are four deities holding their symbols: Ares with his spear, Demeter with her torch, Dionysos with his thyrsos (a wooden staff wrapped around with ivy and vine leaves) and Hermes with his kerykeion (the symbol of the messenger) and his wide hat, the winged petassos. They are sitting at ease and appear to be awaiting the procession.

To the right is Athena with her spear in her right hand, without shield and helmet and with her aegis on her knees. Hephaistos sits beside her, leaning on his club which rests beneath his arm. The next block with the other deities is, as you know, in Athens.

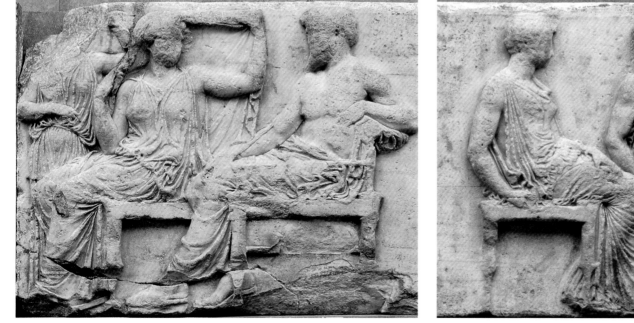

East frieze, block V. Detail.

East frieze, block V. Detail.

The ceremony of giving the peplos is shown in the middle of the east frieze. Five people take part in this. The Priest and a little boy hold the peplos, while to the left stand three women who are carrying the ceremonial objects on their heads and in their hands. Tradition has it that the cloth of the peplos was woven with scenes from the Gigantomachy –on the frieze these scenes were probably painted– a theme that was shown likewise on the east metopes as well as the inner surface of the shield of the Parthenos statue.

There has been much discussion as to who is giving the peplos to whom, the Priest to the boy or the boy to the Priest. Whoever received it then dedicated it to the sacred «Diipetes» statue (fallen from Zeus, or Dias, above) of the goddess within the Erechtheion. Be that as it may, the boy is depicted next to Athena, perhaps a telling piece of evidence. The gods themselves appear to ignore the scene of the giving of the peplos, even though it is the central act and focus of the procession. They sit, as if detached, to the right and left. Unfortunately, here too the faces have been destroyed.

East frieze, block V. Detail.

The ten men who frame the deities represent the eponymous heroes, the ones who gave their names to a corresponding number of tribes of the ancient Athenians. They appear to be discussing matters among themselves. They wear himatia, the chest as a rule exposed, and some lean on staves. Here too, the faces have been badly damaged or destroyed and their state of preservation is mediocre. Even so, the high artistic quality is evident.

East frieze, block IV. Detail.

The same high quality is evident in yet another block from the east end of the frieze, which is today in the **Louvre** in Paris. It shows six maidens, who move from the right toward the centre, and two marshalls, one of whom is holding the sacred box for the sacrifice. With the exception of the one holding a phiale, the maidens proceed with their hands free. These are the weavers of the peplos, the Ergastinai, maidens carefully chosen from noble families. They walk slowly; they wear the peplos which falls in a way suggestive of column flutes. These are among the finest creations of classical Athenian sculpture.

East frieze, block VII, Paris, Louvre.

Some of the blocks have suffered irreparable damage and breakage. There are various reasons for the poor condition in which the Parthenon sculpture has come down to us. While still on the building, the sculpture was subjected through the ages to conflagrations, earthquakes, the bombardment of Morosini's campaign and natural deterioration from rain, wind, frost and atmospheric pollution. To grasp the superb quality of the carving, take a look at the statue of Aphrodite in the east pediment, at the folds of her garment which have remained practically undamaged from the time the statue was made. You can see the marks of the tools used by the sculptors and the marble has retained its translucence while acquiring the reddish brown tone known as a patina, which shows the authenticity and age of sculpture. Unfortunately, shortly before World War II, a clumsy attempt to clean the sculpture in the British Museum appears to have removed this valuable patina from some of the metopes and a few of the pedimental statues.

East pediment, figure M, Aphrodite. Detail.

Do you know how many millions of people have come to the Acropolis and seen me? They have seen me and I have watched them. I always wanted to show the Parthenon to someone, and now with you my wish has been fulfilled. We had to take four promenades together so that you could know the Parthenon. So now I am satisfied and at peace, just as once upon a time the great sculptors of the Golden Age portrayed me in white marble. The misfortunes of the ages brought about the scattering of my sculptured portrayals, once part of a unified whole on the great temple. Yet I believe, that sometime, perhaps quite soon, all these pieces will be united again with the other sculptures that have survived, in an exhibition in the new Acropolis Museum.

That will be a day for joy and celebration for all who love art and understand the message left for the world by the ancient Greeks.

East pediment

A   B   C   D   E   F   G

The east pediment, left half. Drawing J. Carrey 1674, in T. Bowie - D. Thimme,
"The Carrey Drawings of the Parthenon Sculptures", London 1971.

A-C. Helios
and his chariot.
B.M.

D. Dionysos.
B.M.

E-F. Persephone-
Demeter.
B.M.

G. Artemis.
B.M.

The subject of the east pediment was the Birth of Athena from the head of Zeus. The centre of the pediment, however, was missing as early as the first Christian years and its composition is therefore unknown. Scholars have made various suggestions. One problem is whether the central figure of Zeus was shown seated or standing. This in turn affects the position, pose and size of the figures beside him.

K   L   M   O

The east pediment, right half. Drawing J. Carrey, op. cit.

Hera.
A.M.

H. Hephaistos.
A.M.

K-L-M.
Hestia-Dione-Aphrodite.
B.M.

N. Selene.
A.M.

O. Selene's
horse.
B.M.

Elgin broke off all the figures he found in the east pediment. The figures of Selene, Hephaistos and Hera, as well as other fragments, today in the Acropolis Museum, had already fallen when Carrey drew the pediment. They were discovered later on in the excavations.

West pediment

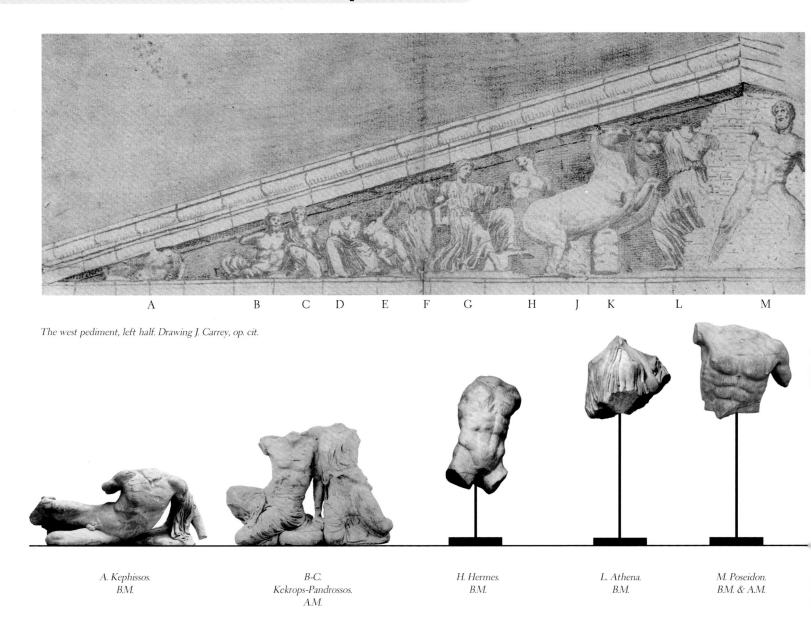

A   B   C   D   E   F   G   H   J   K   L   M

The west pediment, left half. Drawing J. Carrey, op. cit.

A. Kephissos.
B.M.

B-C.
Kekrops-Pandrossos.
A.M.

H. Hermes.
B.M.

L. Athena.
B.M.

M. Poseidon.
B.M. & A.M.

The west pediment, representing the competition between Athena and Poseidon for patronage of Attica, was still preserved practically complete when Carrey made his drawing of it. After this, however, and up to the time of Elgin's pillaging, many statues were broken into pieces. Only Carrey's drawings have enabled archaeologists to reconstruct from fragments the scene in the pediment.

N   O   P   Q   R   S   T   U   V   W

The east pediment, right half. Drawing J. Carrey, op. cit.

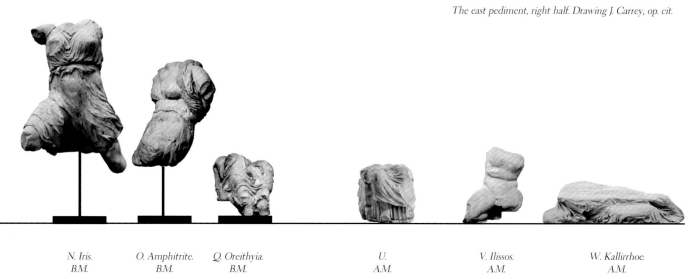

N. Iris.	*O. Amphitrite.*	*Q. Oreithyia.*	*U.*	*V. Ilissos.*	*W. Kallirrhoe.*
B.M.	*B.M.*	*B.M.*	*A.M.*	*A.M.*	*A.M.*

In this case Elgin did not remove all the figures he found. He left in the pediment Kekrops and Pandrossos and also Kallirrhoe. These have been removed recently to the Acropolis Museum. Ilissos and figure U had already fallen from the pediment before Elgin's time. They were found subsequently in the excavations.

135

South metopes

Only the south metopes of the Parthenon were drawn by Carrey. The other metopes had been destroyed by hammering long before, the last north metope toward the west being the only one to have escaped.

Of the thirty-two metopes, twenty three show scenes of the Centauromachy. The nine in the centre have another theme. The composition as a whole has not been convincingly interpreted. The eighteen metopes that are preserved and are shown here in photograph, show scenes of the Centauromachy. We know the sequence of the metopes on the building as well as the form of fourteen metopes from Carrey alone. Thanks to these drawings, specialists are restoring more and more metopes from surviving fragments, including even some of the central metopes.

S.M. 1. In situ.

S.M. 2. B.M.

S.M. 3. B.M.

S.M. 9. B.M.

S.M. 10. Louvre.

S.M. 11. Carrey.

S.M. 17. Carrey.

S.M. 18. Carrey.

S.M. 19 Carrey.

S.M. 25. Carrey.

S.M. 26. B.M.

S.M. 27. B.M.

136

S.M. 4. B.M.

S.M. 5. B.M.

S.M. 6. B.M.

S.M. 7. B.M.

S.M. 8. B.M.

S.M. 12. A.M.

S.M. 13. Carrey.

S.M. 14. Carrey.

S.M. 15. Carrey.

S.M. 16. Carrey.

S.M. 20. Carrey.

S.M. 21. Carrey.

S.M. 22. Carrey.

S.M. 23. Carrey.

S.M. 24. Carrey.

S.M. 28. B.M.

S.M. 29. B.M.

S.M. 30. B.M.

S.M. 31. B.M.

S.M. 32. B.M

East frieze

E.F. I B.M. E.F. II A.M. - Carrey. E.F. III B.M. A.M.

E.F. IV B.M. E.F. V B.M. - A.M.

E.F. VI A.M. B.M.

E.F. VII Louvre. E.F. VIII B.M. E.F. IX A.M. - Carrey

At the middle of the east end is shown the scene of the giving of the peplos, with the gods sitting to the left and right. Men and women are shown walking toward the centre. The east frieze is preserved complete except for the last stone at the northeast corner. This, fortunately, was drawn by Carrey.

The Parthenon frieze, which depicted the Panathenaic procession, is the best preserved unit of all the temple sculpture. Of the original 160 metres of relief, 130 still exist today, divided mainly between the Acropolis and the British museums. Of the 30 metres that are lost, the scenes on some 16 metres are known from Carrey's drawings. The rest remains unknown.

West frieze

W.F. I B.M.   W.F. II B.M.   W.F. III A.M.   W.F. IV A.M.

W.F. V A.M.   W.F. VI A.M.   W.F. VII A.M.   W.F. VIII A.M.

W.F. IX A.M.   W.F. X A.M.   W.F. XI A.M.   W.F. XII A.M.

W.F. XIII A.M.   W.F. XIV A.M.   W.F. XV A.M.   W.F. XVI A.M.

The west frieze shows two marshalls, one at each corner, and between them scenes of riders and horses with great variety of movement. The west frieze is preserved in its entirety.

When Carrey made his drawings of the Parthenon sculpture, the entire frieze was in place, with the exception of the central block of the east end and the six blocks that had been removed in order to insert an equal number of windows. Thirteen years later, the central section of the temple was destroyed by the explosion. While Carrey appears to have drawn whatever he saw, many of the scenes remain unknown because some of his drawings of the north and south sides of the frieze have been lost.

North frieze

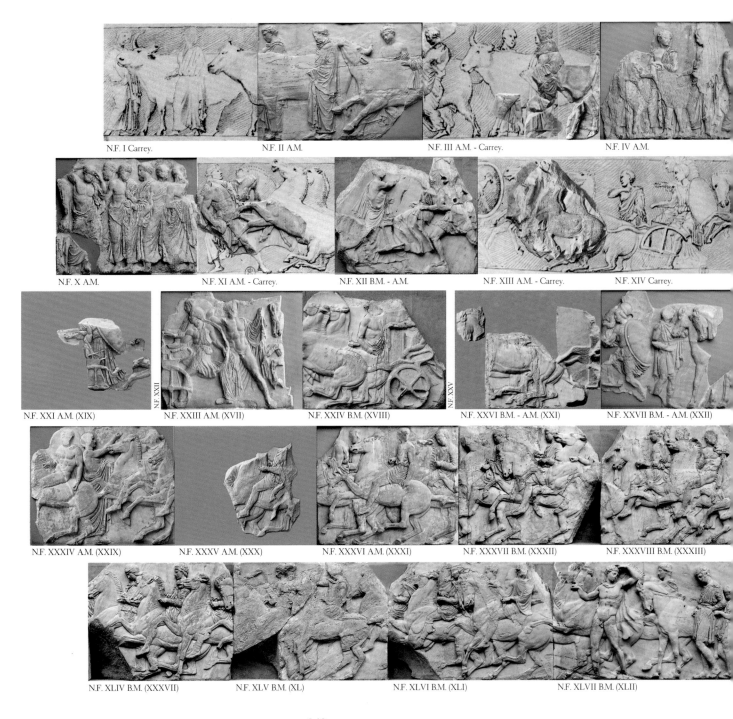

N.F. I Carrey.
N.F. II A.M.
N.F. III A.M. - Carrey.
N.F. IV A.M.

N.F. X A.M.
N.F. XI A.M. - Carrey.
N.F. XII B.M. - A.M.
N.F. XIII A.M. - Carrey.
N.F. XIV Carrey.

N.F. XXI A.M. (XIX)
N.F. XXII
N.F. XXIII A.M. (XVII)
N.F. XXIV B.M. (XVIII)
N.F. XXV
N.F. XXVI B.M. - A.M. (XXI)
N.F. XXVII B.M. - A.M. (XXII)

N.F. XXXIV A.M. (XXIX)
N.F. XXXV A.M. (XXX)
N.F. XXXVI A.M. (XXXI)
N.F. XXXVII B.M. (XXXII)
N.F. XXXVIII B.M. (XXXIII)

N.F. XLIV B.M. (XXXVII)
N.F. XLV B.M. (XL)
N.F. XLVI B.M. (XLI)
N.F. XLVII B.M. (XLII)

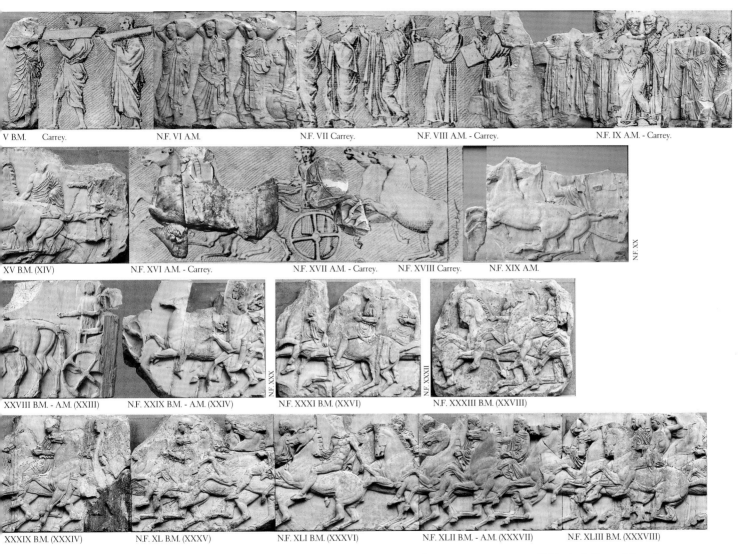

V B.M. Carrey.   N.F. VI A.M.   N.F. VII Carrey.   N.F. VIII A.M. - Carrey.   N.F. IX A.M. - Carrey.

XV B.M. (XIV)   N.F. XVI A.M. - Carrey.   N.F. XVII A.M. - Carrey.   N.F. XVIII Carrey.   N.F. XIX A.M.   N.F. XX

XXVIII B.M. - A.M. (XXIII)   N.F. XXIX B.M. - A.M. (XXIV)   N.F. XXX   N.F. XXXI B.M. (XXVI)   N.F. XXXII   N.F. XXXIII B.M. (XXVIII)

XXXIX B.M. (XXXIV)   N.F. XL B.M. (XXXV)   N.F. XLI B.M. (XXXVI)   N.F. XLII B.M. - A.M. (XXXVII)   N.F. XLIII B.M. (XXXVIII)

The composition of the first section of the north frieze comprises sixty horsemen in groups. This is followed by the apobates' competition with twelve chariots. The sacrificial procession follows with four bulls and four rams. Olive branch bearers, musicians, bearers of water jugs and tray bearers also take part.

Only a third of the Carrrey drawings of the north side are preserved, that showing the eastern section.

Since the other drawings have disappeared, there is no agreement in the international bibliography about the sequence of the frieze blocks on the building.

South frieze

S.F. I A.M.   B.M.   S.F. II A.M.   S.F. III B.M.   S.F. IV A.M.   B.M.

S.F. X A.M.   S.F. XI B.M. - A.M.   S.F. XII B.M.   S.F. XIII B.M.   S.F. XIV A.M.

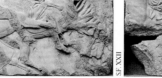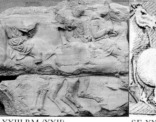

S.F. XX A.M. - Carrey.   S.F. XXI B.M. - A.M.   S.F. XXIII B.M. (XXII)   S.F. XXIV Carrey.   S.F. XXV B.M. (XXIV)

S.F. XXXII B.M. (XXXI)   S.F. XXXIII Carrey.   S.F. XXXIV Carrey.   S.F. XXXV Carrey.

S.F. XLIV B.M. (XL)   S.F. XLV B.M. (XLII)   S.F. XLVI B.M. (XXXVIII)   S.F. XLVII B.M. (XLIV)

V B.M.   S.F. VI B.M.   S.F. VII B.M.   S.F. VIII B.M.   S.F. IX B.M.

XV B.M.   S.F. XVI A.M.   S.F. XVII A.M.   S.F. XVIII A.M.   S.F. XIX B.M.

XXVI B.M. (XXV)   S.F. XXVII Carrey.   S.F. XXVIII Carrey.   S.F. XXIX B.M. - A.M.   S.F. XXX   S.F. XXXI B.M. (XXX)

XXXVI B.M. - Carrey (XXXV).   S.F. XXXVII A.M. Carrey (XXXVI).   S.F. XXXVIII Carrey.   S.F. XXXIX   S.F. XL.   S.F. XLI B.M.   S.F. XLII A.M.   S.F. XLIII B.M. (XXXIX)

The south frieze begins with the marshall who is supervising the contests. Following are sixty riders in groups and ten chariots competing in the race. The next blocks show the sacrificial procession with ten bulls accompanied by their drivers. Taking part also are tray bearers, musicians and bearers of olive branches. Preserved is only a third of Carrey's drawing of the south frieze, showing the middle part. Carrey drew the sculpture as if he were looking at the figures on eye-level, in an effort to correct the distortion resulting from the distance and angle from which he saw them. The striking agreement between the preserved fragments, which have been photographed from directly in front, and the corresponding drawings of Carrey is impressive.

NOTE ON THE DRAWINGS USED IN THE BOOK

J. Carrey saw and drew the sculpture in 1674, before the explosion of the temple in 1687, when the sculpture was still in place on the building. His drawings are of great historical significance. Carrey drew the pediments, the frieze and the south metopes all within fifteen days, viewing them from the ground from amidst houses and walls, continuously changing the viewpoint from which he was drawing them. He could not of course avoid a few small mistakes. None the less his contribution to the study of the Parthenon sculpture is immeasurable. It is unfortunate that not all his drawings have survived. Since the Carrey drawings provide the sole evidence for the form of the statues that are now lost, they have been combined in the Epimetron with contemporary photographs in order to give the fullest picture possible of the aggregate of sculpture that once adorned the great temple.

The drawings of *J. Stuart* and *N. Revett* were made when the sculptures removed by Elgin were still on the monument, at least fifty years after the destruction of 1687. The engravings that were published in England later on were made from these drawings. This work on the Parthenon was of definitive importance for the re-estimation of ancient Greek architecture in western Europe during the 18th century.

The paintings showing the Parthenon restored are the work of three architects, fellows of the cole Nationale Suprieure des Beaux-Arts in Paris: *A. Paccard* (mission of 1845-1846), *M. Lambert* (mission of 1877) and *B. Loviot* (mission of 1879-1880). The paintings of the Erechtheion were drawn by *J. M. Tetaz.* (mission of 1847-1848). From the archaeological standpoint, the more accurate drawings are those of Paccard who measured and drew the Parthenon with great precision. The chief error of Paccard and all the others is that they have restored the Parthenon with an opening in the middle of the roof so that the statue of Athena Parthenos is in the open air. So also the strong colours on the marble parts of the monuments may be termed "artistic license", reflecting rather the Pompeian memories of the artists. Most restorations of the sculptural decoration of the monuments are likewise arbitrary. Lambert and Loviot place the south metopes on the west and east ends respectively. Tetaz draws the frieze of the Parthenon on the Erechtheion.

The work of the architect-painter *K. F. Shinkel* (1825), "A Look at the Golden Age of Greece," reflects a poetic-fantasy approach to the Greek landscape and temples. On the other hand, in "Pheidias and the Parthenon Frieze," the painter *L. Alma Tadema* (1868) has given us a very accurate rendition of the frieze and the marble roof of the opisthodomos as they were in antiquity.

THE NUMBERING OF THE SCULPTURES

The original position of many of the sculptures on the building is unknown; some because they had fallen before Carrey made his drawings, others because Elgin broke them in order to take them and destroyed the evidence for their joining. Thus the specialists differ among themselves as to the identification and position of the sculptures. Of the many scholarly interpretations of the iconography of the sculptural decoration (especially for the pediments and the east metopes), one was chosen and is used by Iris.

In the international bibliography the figures of the pediments are numbered by Latin letters, 24 for the east and 24 for the west.

The metopes of each side have arabic numbers, running from left to right.

The frieze blocks of each side have Latin numbers, running from left to right. The human figures on each side respectively have arabic numbers. For the frieze blocks, the numbering given by I. Jenkins in «The Parthenon Frieze,» London 1994, is followed. The number given by the museum is shown in parenthesis. This is why many of the frieze blocks have two different sets of numbers in the book.